Eat Your Veggies

Glorious Greens, Super Squashes, and a Harvest of Vegetable Delights

By Wendy Esko
Foreword by Gale Jack

One Peaceful World Press
Becket, Massachusetts

For further information on mail-order sales, wholesale or retail dis-
counts, distribution, translations, and foreign rights, please contact
the publisher:

One Peaceful World Press
P.O. Box 10
Leland Road
Becket, MA 01223
U.S.A.

Telephone (413) 623-2322
Fax (413) 623-8827

First Edition: January 1997
10 9 8 7 6 5 4 3 2 1

ISBN 1-882984-24-2
Printed in U.S.A.

Contents

Foreword

A plant-centered diet is increasingly being recognized as the key to health at all levels—personal, social, and planetary. The benefits of a way of eating centered on whole grains and vegetables have been widely documented by a generation of scientific and medical research. The Framingham Heart Study, the China Health Study, the National Institutes of Health research on the macrobiotic approach to cancer, and other major studies on the relation of diet and degenerative disease have all found that people eating a plant-based diet developed less heart disease, cancer, and other chronic illnesses than the usual population.

For twenty-five years, Wendy Esko has been in the forefront of this planetary transformation, as a cook, teacher, author, and mother. Thousands of people—including many leading chefs, holistic health care practitioners, and environmentalists—have studied with Wendy. Thousands of others know her through her many cookbooks and increasingly through articles and recipes on the Internet.

In *Rice Is Nice* and *Soup du Jour*, the first two books in her series of small, affordable cookbooks, Wendy Esko presented many delicious recipes for whole grains and soups that could be prepared day to day, season to season, to create health in the home and family. In *Eat Your Veggies*, the first macrobiotic cookbook devoted entirely to vegetables, she presents over one hundred tasty and creative ways to serve leafy greens, squashes and other round vegetables, and root vegetables.

As natural farmer Masanobu Fukuoka, author of *The One Straw Revolution*, observed during a visit to the Kushi Institute, the secret to a happy life, especially harmonious relations between man and woman, is a wide variety of fresh vegetables, properly prepared and attractively presented. If there are not enough vegetables in the daily menu, he explained, family members are likely to binge and seek foods outside the home, thereby reducing natural polarity and attraction between the mother and father, as well as children, grandparents, and other household members. Grains, beans, and soup are indispensable to daily health, but it is vegetables that hold the meal together and determine whether it is a symphony or a performance of untuned instruments.

As part of a balanced diet and lifestyle, the recipes in this book will go a long way to help you preserve your own health and vitality, as well as that of your family and the earth as a whole.

This cookbook will find a treasured place in my kitchen, as I trust it will in yours. I look forward eagerly to *Full of Beans*, Wendy's next book in her series for One Peaceful World Press.

Gale Jack
Becket, Massachusetts
October 1996

Gale Jack is a cooking teacher at the Kushi Institute, director of the Women's Macrobiotic Society, and author of the best-selling cookbook Amber Waves of Grain *(Japan Publications).*

Introduction

Nowhere is the bounty of nature more apparent than in the world of vegetables. Nature continually supplies us with a vast selection of vegetables, all in different shapes, sizes, colors, and tastes. Each vegetable provides a unique balance of nutrients and energy.

Vegetables are the perfect complement to brown rice and other whole grains. Together they comprise the foundation of a healthful natural diet. Cooking makes the nutrients in vegetables more readily available. Vegetables contain cellulose, which can be difficult to digest. Raw vegetable eaters such as cows and sheep have special digestive organs that break down tough plant fibers. Humans lack these digestive organs and thus rely on cooking to soften the tough fiber in plants. In this sense, we can regard cooking as a form of pre-digestion.

Through cooking, we change the energy of vegetables and other foods. Cooking vegetables for a short time over a high flame accelerates their yin, upward or expanding energy. Cooking vegetables for a longer time over a low flame concentrates their nutrients and energy, thus making them more yang. Within these two opposite approaches to cooking, there are generally five varieties of expanding and contracting energy.

Upward, or expanding energy is accelerated by quickly steaming vegetables. Steam is produced by the boiling of water, and moves actively in an upward direction. Leafy greens are also charged by upward energy, and are often cooked this way. Pickling involves the breakdown and release of energy through fermentation. Pickling, and especially quick-pickling, is also classified in the upward energy category. Marinating also causes vegetables to release energy, and can be included in the same category as quick-steaming and pickling.

Blanching, quick-sautéing, stir-frying, and deep-frying utilize intense heat and energy, and accelerate the actively expanding energy in vegetables and other foods. When foods are cooked this way, they are more strongly energized than steamed or pickled foods.

Five Stages of Cooking

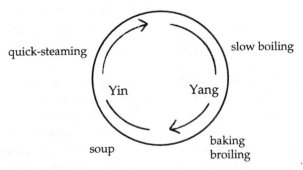

blanching, quick sautéing

quick-steaming

slow boiling

Yin   Yang

soup

baking
broiling

In contrast to these energy-activating methods, are cooking styles that utilize a lower flame and more time in order to concentrate the energy in foods. Nishime, or waterless cooking, is an example. In Nishime, vegetables such as squash, daikon, and carrots are boiled until the water evaporates. This method causes the dish to have more downward or stabilzing energy. Slowly boiling vegetables over a low flame thus produces a more yang effect.

Some cooking methods produce even more concentrated energy. Examples are baking, broiling, and pressure cooking. Baking and broiling make vegetables dry and contracted. Baking takes place in a yang, enclosed space (an oven), and causes vegetables and other foods to have drying and tightening effects. Pressure cooking also concentrates energy in an inward direction. Because these methods produce strongly contractive effects, we don't use them as often as the lighter, quicker methods of cooking. I usually don't pressure cook vegetables, but reserve this method for brown rice and other whole grains. Usually I serve baked or broiled vegetables only on occasion.

In between these strongly yin and strongly yang methods of cooking is another cooking method. In this method we boil vegetables and other foods in plenty of water. This method is known as *soup*. By adjusting ingredients and cooking times, soups can be made to produce lighter, more expansive effects, or heavier and more concentrated effects. Soups that are quickly prepared with fewer ingredients are generally more yin or expansive, while those cooked for a longer time with more ingredients generally have more yang or concentrated energy.

For the most part, vegetables have lighter, less concentrated energy than do grains and beans. Since we utilize vegetables to balance the energy of grains and beans, quicker, lighter cooking methods are generally preferred. Also, among vegetables themselves, we can identify three energetic categories. Root vegetables, such as carrots, turnips, and daikon, grow below the ground and are strongly charged with contracting energy. Round vegetables, such as squash, cabbage, and onions, have a more evenly balanced energy. Leafy greens such as daikon, carrot, turnip, and mustard greens are strongly charged with upward, expanding energy. Because we use vegetables to balance grains and beans, which have strong concentrated energy, we generally choose a higher proportion of leafy greens in our daily diets.

However, in nature, and in the vegetable world especially, diversity is the rule, not the exception. Translated into the daily selection of vegetables, the rule of diversity means that we need ample variety. Day to day, week to week, and month to month, we need a wide selection of vegetables from each of these categories. As everyone knows, vegetables and other foods that are grown organically—without pesticides or fertilizers—are superior to those grown chemically. However, because organic vegetables are not widely available, we may need to rely on non-organic produce in order to sustain adequate variety in our daily selection.

As you try the recipes in this book, you will notice that vegetables such as tomatoes, potatoes, green and red peppers, and eggplant are used only rarely or not at all. These vegetables belong to the nightshade family, and originated in tropical or equatorial zones. One of the most important principles of healthful, ecological eating is to base one's diet on foods that have originated in one's climatic zone. Therefore, in this book, we rely primarily on vegetables that are native to the temperate regions of the world.

Washing and Cutting Vegetables

Washing and cutting your vegetables properly is the secret to making delicious and appetizing vegetable dishes. With practice, your washing skills and knife technique will approach that of a master chef. Below are some pointers that can help you along the way.

Washing Root or Ground Vegetables

Vegetables other than leafy greens can be scrubbed with a natural-bristle vegetable brush to properly remove soil while keeping the skin intact. Place the vegetables in the sink and run cold water over them. Gently but firmly scrub with the vegetable brush, making sure not to damage the nutrient-rich skin. Green cabbage, most types of lettuce, and Chinese cabbage require removing part or all of the leaves from the core and washing the leaves individually under cold water. Vegetables that have waxed skins require peeling to remove the skin and are then simply rinsed under cold water.

Vegetables such as leeks need to be split lengthwise down the center and each leaf needs to be carefully washed to remove soil. The root portion of leeks, scallions, and chives can be held under cold running water and scrubbed firmly to remove soil. Vegetables such as burdock have a rather delicate skin that can easily be damaged by scrubbing too firmly. The skin is naturally brown or dark brown. If the skin has turned white when you are finished scrubbing, you have scrubbed too hard.

Cucumbers, if unwaxed, can be washed in the same manner as roots. If waxed, remove the skin, and rinse under cold water before using. For root vegetables with the greens still attached, remove the green portion and wash as you would other leafy greens. The root can be washed as above. Onions can first be peeled and then rinsed quickly under cold water until clean. If vegetables that require peeling are heavily caked with soil, it is a good idea to first scrub the vegetable with the skin left on before peeling and rinsing under cold water. Fresh shiitake and other mushrooms can simply be rinsed thoroughly by hand under cold water, instead of using a vegetable brush.

Washing Leafy Greens

Before washing greens, sort through them to remove any yellowed or damaged leaves. Next, place the greens in a large bowl or pot and completely cover with cold water. Let them soak for several seconds. Then wash by swishing the leaves around in the water. Remove the leaves and pour off the water. Now take one leaf and wash it thoroughly under cold running water to remove any remaining soil or dust. With tightly curled leaves, such as kale, make sure to gently unfurl them while rinsing to remove any matter hidden from sight. Wash each leaf individually under cold water until completely clean.

Watercress may have small shells in it, so it is important to wash each leaf thoroughly. Celery sometimes has soil caked between the ribs that run up the stalk. To remove it, take a vegetable brush and lightly scrub. Leafy greens such as collards, cabbage, or Chinese cabbage, which have smoother leaves, generally do not require as much effort to wash as vegetables with jagged edges.

Turnip, rutabaga, radish, and daikon tops sometimes have sandy soil attached to them. Rinsing the whole bunch in a pot once or twice is not sufficient to remove the soil. Make sure to rinse each leaf as well under cold water. Some greens, such as lettuce, cabbage, or Chinese cabbage, require removal of the leaves from the core or stem so that each can be washed separately. Broccoli can also be difficult to clean, as it has hundreds of tiny florets tightly packed together. It may require soaking for several minutes before washing and rinsing. Once the greens are thoroughly washed, place them in a colander and let them drain before slicing or cooking whole. String beans and peas are very easy to clean and can simply be rinsed individually or in a colander under cold water.

It is better not to cut vegetables before you wash them. Once you slice a vegetable, there is more exposed surface area from which nutrients and flavor can escape.

The Art of Cutting

Choosing the right cuts for your vegetable dishes is very important both in terms of flavor and appearance. In macrobiotic cooking, we often cut vegetables on an angle (so as to balance expanding and contracting energies), which makes it possible to create a large variety of beautiful cuts. However, at times we also cut vegetables straight across, as we do with cuts such as rounds, rectangles, and diced vegetables.

When several styles of cutting are combined in one dish, it is better to keep the cuts generally uniform in terms of size and thickness. Also, when you cut vegetables in large chunks, it is better to keep them bite-sized so that it is easier to eat them. With continual practice, your cutting technique and speed will improve, so do not be overwhelmed if vegetable cutting seems difficult at first.

The proper use of your knife is essential in smooth and effortless cutting. Grip the knife handle firmly with either hand. If you are right-handed, curl your index, middle, ring, and little fingers firmly around the right side of the handle. Rest your thumb firmly against the left side of the handle. Grip firmly with all of your fingers, but not too tightly. Holding your knife too tightly can make your arm tire quickly, especially if you have a lot of cutting to do. It can also interfere with your ability to make smooth, clean cuts. Actually, the thumb and index finger can be used to apply the most pressure. The other fingers can be used to balance the handle, thus making knife control easier.

When holding the vegetables that are being cut, curl your fingers in slightly at the first joint. This prevents or reduces the chance of cutting yourself while slicing. Tilt the blade slightly away from your fingers, with the upper portion of the blade resting gently against the middle or end joint of your middle finger. Place the blade on the vegetable and slide it, firmly but gently, forward through the vegetable, with a slight downward pressure.

Cut with the entire length of the blade. It is best not to saw or push down too hard to the extent that the knife tears through the vegetable. This produces jagged slices that are not so attractive or balanced.

Sometimes, when slicing long vegetables or leafy greens, we use a technique known as the "drawing motion." In this method, we use only the tip of the knife. Place the tip on the vegetable and draw the blade back toward you until the entire length of it is cut.

The most commonly used methods for cutting vegetables are illustrated in the diagram below.

13

1
Steamed and Boiled Vegetables

Steaming accelerates the upward, expanding energy of vegetables and other foods. Quickly steamed greens can be eaten daily as a perfect counterpoint to the concentrated energy in whole grains and beans. Depending on the strength of the flame and the amount of time used in cooking, boiling can produce either more activating or stablilizing effects. Blanching, in which we dip vegetables into boiling water, produces very activating effects. Vegetable Nabe, in which vegetables and other foods are quickly cooked in boiling water, also activates energy. On the other hand, slow-boiling and simmering, in which a lower flame is utilized, produces more concentrated energy and a stabilizing effect. Both energy-activating and energy-concentrating methods are illustrated in this chapter.

There are many types of steamers sold in natural food stores and kitchen specialty shops. There are bamboo steamers with layers of baskets that can be stacked one on top of the other. These are nice if you want to steam two or three vegetables at a time. There are inexpensive stainless steel steamers that fit in almost any size pot. Other styles of stainless steel and ceramic steamers are also available. Any type will do. If you do not have a steamer, you can simply place enough water in a pot to barely cover the bottom, heat the water, and add the vegetables. Then cover and steam.

When steaming vegetables, it is usually better to choose vegetables with sweeter tastes such as kale, broccoli, onion, corn, carrot, Chinese cabbage, bok choy, and squash. Steaming causes them to retain their flavor and become sweeter. When steamed, bitter tasting vegetables such as parsley, watercress, carrot top, endive, chicory, dandelion, escarole, burdock, Italian broccoli, and others become more bitter as there is no water for their bitter flavor to be released in.

Steamed Greens

2 cups greens, chopped
water

Place 1 to 2 inches of water in a steamer pot, cover, and bring to a boil. Place the steamer basket on or in the pot, depending on the type of steamer you have. Place the chopped vegetables in the steamer, cover, and steam for 2 to 3 minutes or until tender but still bright green. Remove and place in a serving dish.

Steamed Winter Squash

2 cups buttercup, butternut, or other winter squash,
sliced in chunks
water

Place the water in the steamer pot, cover, and bring to a boil. Add the squash, cover, and steam for 2 to 4 minutes (size of chunks will determine cooking time) or until tender. Remove and place in a serving dish.

Steamed Summer Squash

2 yellow summer squash, cut in 1/2 inch thick rounds
water

Place the water in the steamer pot, cover, and bring to a boil. Add the squash, cover, and steam for 2 to 3 minutes. Remove and place in a serving dish.

Steamed Stuffed Squash

    1 buttercup or acorn squash, halved and seeds removed
    1 1/2 cups leftover cooked millet, rice, barley, bulgur, or cous cous
    1/4 cup onion, diced
    1/4 cup carrot, diced
    1 Tbsp celery, diced
    2 Tbsp dry-roasted pumpkin, sunflower, or sesame seeds
    1/2 tsp shoyu
    water, for steaming

Place the leftover cooked grain and the vegetables in a mixing bowl. Add the shoyu and mix thoroughly. Place the stuffing in the hollow center of the squash halves until full. Place 1 to 2 inches of water in the steamer pot. Cover and bring to a boil. Place the stuffed squash halves in the steamer basket, cover, and steam several minutes until tender. Remove and place on a serving platter. To serve, slice each squash half in half. You may serve as is or with a natural sauce or gravy.

Other stuffings may be substituted for the above, including chopped or ground seitan and vegetables, chopped or ground tempeh and vegetables, and grain, vegetables, and sauerkraut.

Steamed Whole Onions
with Shiitake-Kuzu Gravy

    12 small white boiling onions, peeled and left whole
    water, for steaming onions
    5 to 6 shiitake mushrooms, soaked, stems removed, and

chopped
1 1/2 cups water
2 tsp kuzu, diluted in 3 tsp water
1 1/2 to 2 tsp shoyu
1 Tbsp parsley, minced
1/2 tsp dark or light sesame oil (optional)

Place 1 to 2 inches of water in a steamer pot, cover, and bring to a boil. Remove cover and place the whole onions in the steamer. Cover the steamer and steam the onions 3 to 5 minutes or until tender. Remove and place in a serving dish. To prepare the gravy, place the oil in a skillet and heat. Add the shiitake and sauté for 1 to 2 minutes. Add the water and diluted kuzu. Stir constantly until the sauce becomes thick and translucent. Add the shoyu, reduce the flame to medium-low, and simmer 3 to 5 minutes. Pour the gravy over the onions and then sprinkle the parsley on top. Serve.

Boiled Whole Greens

The advantage of boiling vegetables in their whole form is that they retain more of their flavor and nutrients. This method is particularly nice for watercress, parsley, kale, Chinese cabbage, radish greens, turnip greens, and such. If the stem of the vegetable is tough, simply slice off the lower tough end from the leaf and boil it separately. The cooking time will vary depending on the thickness of the vegetable. Most greens take between 1 to 2 minutes. Excessive boiling (beyond 3 minutes) destroys vitamins and greatly diminishes the vegetable's bright green color.

1 bunch watercress, washed
water

Place about 1 inch of water in a pot, cover, and bring to a boil. Remove the cover and place the watercress in the pot. Boil for 50 to 60 seconds. Remove and drain. If you want to stop the cooking action immediately to preserve the rich green color, simply rinse for several seconds under cold water. Chop if desired and place on a serving plate. The greens can be served as is, with a dressing, or with a few roasted seeds mixed in.

Blanched Chopped Greens

> 1 small bunch kale, washed and chopped in 1 to 2 inch
>   lengths
> water

Place 1 inch of water in a pot, cover, and bring to a boil. Remove the cover and place the kale in the pot. Cover and cook for 1 1/2 to 2 minutes. Remove, drain, and place in a serving dish.

Vegetable Green Rolls

> 6 to 8 medium Chinese cabbage leaves, washed and left
>   whole
> 1 bunch watercress, washed and left whole
> 1 medium carrot, sliced in lengthwise strips
> water
> 1 tsp umeboshi paste (optional)

Place 1 to 2 inches of water in a pot, cover, and bring to a boil. While the water is coming to a boil, slice the carrot into thin lengthwise strips. Place the carrot strips in the water, cover, and bring to a boil again. Boil for 1 1/2 to 2 minutes. Remove and place in a strainer to drain. Place on a plate. Place the Chinese cabbage in the same water, cover, and boil 1 minute. Remove, drain, and place on a plate to cool off. Next, place the watercress in the water and boil 50 to 60 seconds. Remove, place in a strainer, and rinse under cold water for 10 seconds. Place on a plate.

Place a bamboo sushi mat on your cutting board. Place 1 Chinese cabbage leaf on the mat. Next, place another leaf on the mat so that it slightly overlaps the first, and with the thicker end of the leaf running in the opposite direction as the first leaf. Take several more leaves and place them, overlapping and running in alternate directions from the first leaves, on top. Take 2 or 3 thin carrot strips and place them lengthwise across the entire length of the first cabbage leaf. Then take half of the watercress and place it evenly across the length of the carrot . Use your knife to trim any leaves or carrot that hang over the edge of the mat and place the trimmings evenly on top of the watercress.

Now roll the mat up, just as you would if you were making sushi, by placing your fingers on top of the watercress and your thumbs underneath the mat. Pull the mat up slightly with your index fingers and thumbs. With your other fingers, tuck the cabbage leaves under as you roll them up. Continue rolling forward, pressing firmly with your fingers and pulling the mat back toward you as you roll, so as not to roll the mat up inside with the vegetables. When you finish, you should have a tightly rolled cylinder of leaves. After you finish, roll the mat completely around the cylinder and pick it up with your hands. Gently squeeze several times to remove excess water.

Remove the roll and place it on your cutting board. Slice the roll in half. Next, slice each half in half, so that you have 4 pieces. Then slice each quarter in half. You should now have 8 slices of green rolls. Arrange the rolls on a serving platter with the sliced side facing up.

Repeat the above steps, making another roll, using up the remaining vegetables. Slice and arrange on the platter. Take a small amount of umeboshi paste and place a small dab on top of each roll. Serve.

Vegetable Sushi

This dish is a variation of the previous recipe but uses nori sea vegetable as a wrapping for the vegetables. The greens that are most suitable for this are watercress, mustard greens, turnip greens, kale, or spinach. As with green rolls, carrot or daikon strips or pickles can be rolled up in the center to make a more colorful dish. I find this a great way to use leftover greens.

1 bunch mustard greens, washed and left whole
2 to 3 sheets nori, toasted
1/4 cup tan sesame seeds, roasted
1 to 2 tsp shiso condiment
water

Place 1 to 2 inches of water in a pot, cover, and bring to a boil. Place the mustard greens in the water, cover, and boil 1 1/2 minutes. Remove and rinse quickly under cold water. Gently squeeze the greens to remove excess water and place on a plate.

Place a sushi mat on the cutting board and place 1 sheet of nori on top of it. Divide the mustard greens into 2 to 3 equal portions. Take one portion and place it on top of the nori, spreading it out across the length of the nori, forming a line about 2 inches wide. Sprinkle a teaspoonful of seeds all across the greens, followed by about 1/4 teaspoon of shiso powder. Roll the mat around the vegetables as in the above recipe. When completely rolled up, wrap the mat around the nori roll and gently squeeze out excess water while sealing the nori around the greens. Remove the mat and place the nori roll on the cutting board. Slice the roll in half. Slice each half in half and then each quarter in half. You now have eight pieces of nori roll. Place on end on a platter. Repeat the above steps until all vegetables have been rolled up and sliced.

Boiled Salad with Tofu Dressing

1 cup broccoli florets
1/2 cup cauliflower florets
1/4 cup carrot, sliced in matchsticks or thin diagonals
1/4 cup red radish, halved or quartered
1/4 cup yellow wax beans, sliced in 1 to 2 inch lengths
water

Place 1 to 2 inches of water in a pot, cover, and bring to a boil. Place the wax beans in the water and boil 2 minutes. Remove, drain, and place in a mixing bowl. Next, place the carrot in the boiling water and boil 1 1/2 to 2 minutes. Remove, drain, and place in the mixing bowl. Boil the cauliflower for 2 to 2 1/2 minutes; the broccoli for 2 minutes; and the red radishes for 1 to 1 1/2 minutes. After draining, place in the mixing bowl and mix. Place in a serving bowl. Prepare the dressing as follows:

Tofu Dressing

> 1/2 lb firm style tofu, rinsed
> 1/2 cup water
> 1 Tbsp onion, finely grated
> 1 1/2 to 2 Tbsp umeboshi vinegar
> 2 Tbsp chives, scallion, or parsley, chopped fine

Place a hand food mill over a bowl or suribachi. Purée the tofu through the mill. Remove the mill. Add the water, onion, umeboshi vinegar, and chives to the tofu purée and mix thoroughly. Serve the dressing on the side with the salad or mix it in with the vegetables just before serving.

Boiled Salad with Pumpkin Seed Dressing

> 1 cup broccoli florets
> 1 cup cauliflower florets
> 1/4 cup carrot, sliced in thin diagonals
> 1/4 cup red radish, halved or quartered
> 1/2 cup Chinese cabbage, sliced in 1 inch squares
> water, for boiling vegetables
> 1/2 cup pumpkin seeds, dry-roasted
> 1 1/2 umeboshi plums
> 2 Tbsp parsley, chives, or scallion, minced
> water, for dressing

Place 2 inches of water in a saucepan and bring to a boil.

Add the Chinese cabbage, bring to a boil, and boil 1 minute. Remove and place in a colander or strainer to drain. Place in a serving bowl. Next, boil the carrot for 2 minutes. Drain and place in the serving bowl. Next, boil the cauliflower for 2 1/2 minutes, drain, and place in the serving bowl. Next, boil the broccoli for 2 minutes, drain, and place in the serving bowl. Finally, boil the radish for 1 minute, drain, and place in the serving bowl. Toss to mix.

Place the roasted pumpkin seeds in a suribachi and grind until half-crushed. Remove the pit from the umeboshi and hand-grind with the seeds. Next, add the parsley, chives, or scallion and grind with the seeds and umeboshi. Add a little water at a time to the mixture until you have the consistency you desire for the dressing. It should not be too thick or too watery. If you desire a more salty-sour flavor, adjust the taste by adding a little umeboshi vinegar. Place in a serving dish so that each person can spoon the dressing over their salad. Roasted sesame seeds can be used instead of pumpkin seeds for a different flavor and color.

Carrot, Carrot Tops, and Sesame Seeds

> 1 cup carrot, sliced in thin rounds
> 1 cup carrot tops, chopped fine
> 1/4 cup tan sesame seeds, roasted
> 1 tsp shoyu
> water

Place 1 inch water in a pot, cover, and bring to a boil. Place the sliced carrot in the pot, cover, and boil for 2 minutes. Remove, drain, and place in a mixing bowl. Place the carrot tops in the pot and boil for 1 minute. Remove, drain, and place in the mixing bowl. Place the sesame seeds in a suribachi and grind until about half-crushed. Add the shoyu and grind again to thoroughly mix in the shoyu. Mix the sesame seeds with the vegetables and place in a serving bowl.

Carrot Tops with Pumpkin Seeds

2 cups carrot tops, chopped fine
1/4 cup pumpkin seeds, roasted
1 tsp shoyu
water

Place 1 inch of water in a pot, cover, and bring to a boil.
Boil the carrot tops for 1 minute. Remove and drain. Place the
pumpkin seeds in a suribachi and grind until almost completely crushed. Add the shoyu and grind again to thoroughly mix. Place the carrot tops in the suribachi with the seeds
and mix thoroughly. Place in a serving bowl.

Burdock and Sesame Seed Dressing

2 cups burdock, shaved or cut in matchsticks
2 tsp brown rice vinegar
water
1/4 tan sesame seeds, roasted
1 tsp shoyu
1 tsp parsley, minced

Place 1 inch of water in a pot with the vinegar, cover, and
bring to a boil. Add the burdock, cover, and boil for 2 to 3
minutes until tender. Grind the sesame seeds in a suribachi
until half-crushed. Add the shoyu and grind to mix thoroughly. Add 1/4 cup of the burdock cooking water and mix, making a thick pasty dressing. Mix the burdock in with the sesame dressing and place in a serving bowl.

Crushed Burdock with Sesame Vinaigrette

2 medium burdock roots, washed
1 cup water, for soaking burdock
1 Tbsp brown rice vinegar, for soaking burdock

1 cup water, for cooking burdock
1 Tbsp mirin (sweet cooking rice wine)
1 Tbsp shoyu
1/4 cup tan sesame seeds, roasted
2 to 2 1/2 Tbsp water
1 Tbsp brown rice syrup
2 Tbsp brown rice vinegar
1/2 tsp shoyu

Pound and crush the burdock with a wooden pestle or mallet until it becomes slightly flattened and fibrous. Cut the crushed roots in 2 inch lengths and place them in a bowl. Pour 1 cup water and 1 tablespoon vinegar over the burdock, mix, and let sit 1 hour, mixing occasionally.

Place 1 cup water, mirin, and 1 tablespoonful of shoyu in a saucepan. Add the burdock, cover, and bring to a boil. Reduce the flame to medium-low and simmer 3 to 5 minutes until tender. Remove, rinse, and drain. Grind the sesame seeds in a suribachi until half-crushed. Place the remaining water, rice syrup, vinegar, and shoyu in a pot and heat. Pour the mixture over the crushed seeds and mix. Toss the burdock with the dressing, mixing thoroughly. Let sit for 2 hours and serve.

Green Beans with Sesame-Miso Dressing

2 cups (1 lb) green beans, stems removed and sliced in 2 inch lengths
water, for boiling beans
2 Tbsp red miso (may substitute barley or yellow miso)
1/4 cup tan sesame seeds, roasted
2 to 3 Tbsp water
1 Tbsp mirin (optional)
2 Tbsp brown rice syrup

Place 1 inch of water in a pot, cover, and bring to a boil. Add the beans, cover, and simmer 2 to 3 minutes until tender. Remove, rinse, and drain. Place the water, miso, mirin, and syrup in a saucepan and simmer 2 minutes. Grind the sesame seeds in a suribachi until half-crushed. Add the miso mixture and mix thoroughly. Add the beans to the sesame dressing and mix. Place in a serving bowl.

Boiled Kale with Peanut-Mustard Sauce

   1 small bunch kale, washed and chopped
   water, for boiling kale
   2 Tbsp unsalted organic peanut butter
   1/4 cup water
   1 to 2 tsp natural mustard
   1 tsp shoyu

Place 1 inch water in a pot, cover, and bring to a boil. Add the kale, cover, and boil 2 minutes. Remove, drain, and place in a serving bowl. Place the peanut butter, natural mustard, and shoyu in a suribachi and grind to a smooth paste. Add the water and purée again. Let the dressing sit for 1 hour and then place in a serving dish. Spoon over the boiled greens.

Summer Nishime (Waterless Cooking)

   1 strip kombu, 1 inch by 2 inches after soaking
   1 cup cabbage, cut in 1 inch squares
   1/2 cup carrot, cut in bite-sized chunks
   1/2 cup sweet corn, removed from the cob
   water
   several drops shoyu

Place the kombu in a heavy pot. Layer the cabbage, sweet corn, and carrot on top. Add 1/2 inch water. Cover and bring to a boil over a high flame. Reduce the flame to medium-low and simmer 5 to 7 minutes. Add shoyu, cover, and simmer for 4 to 5 minutes longer. Remove cover, turn the flame to high, and cook off most of the remaining liquid. When there is just a small amount of liquid left, mix the vegetables. Place in a serving dish.

Winter Nishime

  1 strip kombu, 1 inch by 2 inches after soaking
  2 shiitake mushrooms, soaked, stems removed, and
     quartered
  1/2 cup daikon, cut in thick rounds and quartered
  1/2 cup carrot, cut in bite-sized chunks
  1/4 cup celery, cut in thick diagonals
  1/2 cup buttercup or butternut squash, cut in 1 inch
     chunks
  1/2 cup Brussels sprouts, halved
  1/4 cup burdock, sliced on a thin diagonal
  water, including kombu and shiitake soaking water
  several drops shoyu

Place the kombu in a heavy pot. Layer the vegetables on top of the kombu in the following order: shiitake, daikon, celery, Brussels sprouts, squash, burdock, and carrot. Add 1/2 inch water, cover, and bring to a boil. Reduce the flame to medium-low and simmer about 10 minutes. Add several drops of shoyu, cover, and simmer another 5 minutes until the vegetables are tender. Remove the cover, turn the flame to high, and cook off most of the remaining liquid. Mix the vegetables and place in a serving dish.

Whole Onions with Miso-Kuzu Sauce

  4 to 5 medium-sized onions
  1 strip kombu, 1 inch by 2 inches after soaking, diced
  1 tsp miso, puréed with a little water
  1 Tbsp parsley, minced
  2 cups water
  2 tsp kuzu, diluted

Make 1/4 inch slits in the top of each onion to create a pinwheel effect. Place the kombu in a heavy pot. Place the onions in the pot, standing with the slit side up. Add the water. Place about 1/4 teaspoon puréed miso on top of each onion. Cover and bring to a boil. Reduce the flame to medium-low and simmer about 20 to 25 minutes or until tender. Make sure not to over-cook the onions as they will fall apart. Scrape the miso off each onion and place it in the cooking water. Remove the onions and place them in a serving dish. Add the kuzu to the cooking water, stirring constantly, until the liquid is thick. Taste the sauce. If it is not salty enough, add a little more puréed miso and cook 2 minutes. Pour the sauce over the onions and garnish with minced parsley.

Red Radishes with Umeboshi-Kuzu Sauce

   2 bunches red radishes with greens
   3 umeboshi plums
   2 cups water, for cooking radishes
   2 tsp kuzu, diluted
   1 cup water, for cooking radish greens

Place the radishes, umeboshi, and 2 cups of water in a saucepan, cover, and bring to a boil. Reduce the flame to medium-low and simmer 5 minutes until tender. Remove the plums and set aside. They may be used later in another dish. Remove the radishes and place in a serving bowl. Add the kuzu to the cooking liquid, stirring constantly, until thick. Pour the sauce over the radishes.

In another saucepan, place 1 cup water, cover, and bring to a boil. Place the whole radish greens in the pan, cover, and cook for 1 minute. Remove and slice. Place the greens in the center of the bowl with the red radishes so that they are surrounded by the radishes and sauce. Serve.

Tempeh and Vegetable Stuffed Cabbage Rolls

1 lb tempeh, cut in 4 to 5 equal chunks, about 2 inches by 3 inches
4 to 5 whole cabbage leaves
1/3 cup sauerkraut
1/2 cup carrot, cut in matchsticks
1/2 cup onion, cut in half-moons
1 cup green string beans, stems removed and left whole
sesame oil, for browning tempeh (optional)
2 cups water
2 tsp kuzu, diluted
several drops shoyu
small amount of water, for steaming cabbage leaves
4 to 5 toothpicks, for securing the cabbage rolls
1 Tbsp parsley, minced, for garnish

Place a small amount of sesame oil in a skillet and heat. Add the tempeh chunks and pan-fry each side until golden. Remove and place on a plate. Place a small amount of water in a pot, cover, and bring to a boil. Place the cabbage leaf in the water, cover, and cook 1 minute to soften slightly to make rolling easier. Remove and place on a plate.

Make a V-shaped cut in the thick base of each cabbage leaf and remove. Save and put in the rolls with the other vegetables.

Take a cabbage leaf and place a piece of tempeh on it near the thick base of the leaf. Next, place a small amount of carrot, onion, sauerkraut, and string bean on top of the tempeh. Fold the sides of the leaf over the tempeh and vegetables and roll it forward to make a roll. Secure with a toothpick. Repeat until all ingredients are rolled in the leaves. You should now have 4 to 5 cabbage rolls.

Place the rolls in a cast iron or heavy skillet. Add enough water to half-cover the rolls. Season the liquid with shoyu for a mildly salty taste. Cover and bring to a boil. Reduce the flame to medium-low and simmer about 10 minutes or until the rolls are very tender. Remove the rolls and take out the toothpicks. Place in a serving dish. Add the kuzu to the cooking water, stirring constantly, until thick. Pour the sauce over the rolls and garnish with minced parsley.

Boiled Root Vegetables and Tops

For this dish we use the entire vegetable including the green top and root. You may use daikon and tops, red radish and tops, carrot and tops, turnip and tops, rutabaga and turnip tops, and dandelion roots and tops.

1 medium daikon and daikon greens
water
several drops shoyu

Chop the daikon greens in 1 inch lengths and place on a plate. Cut the daikon root in thin half-moons or quarters. Place the root in a saucepan. Add enough water to half-cover. Cover the pan and bring to a boil. Reduce the flame to medium-low and simmer 4 to 5 minutes. Place the daikon greens in the pot on top of the root. Add several drops of shoyu. Cover and simmer 2 minutes until the greens are tender but still bright green. Mix and place in a serving bowl.

Dried Daikon and Vegetables

1 cup dried daikon, rinsed and soaked
1 cup onion, cut in thin half-moons
1/2 cup carrot, cut in matchsticks
1/2 cup sweet corn, removed from cob
4 to 5 shiitake mushrooms, soaked, stems removed, and
 sliced thin
1 strip kombu, 1 inch by 2 inches after soaking, diced or
 sliced in strips
water, including kombu and shiitake soaking water
several drops shoyu

Place the kombu and shiitake in a skillet. Layer the vegetables on top in the following order: onion, corn, carrot, and dried daikon. Add enough water to cover the carrot. Cover and bring to a boil. Reduce the flame to medium-low and simmer for 25 minutes. Add several drops shoyu, cover, and simmer another 5 minutes. Remove the cover, turn the flame to high, and cook off most of the remaining liquid. When there is only a small amount left, mix the vegetables and place in a serving bowl.

Corn on the Cob

> 4 to 5 ears sweet corn, husks and silk removed, left
>   whole
> water
> 2 small umeboshi plums

Place the corn in a pot and add water to half-cover. Cover and bring to a boil. Reduce the flame to medium-low and simmer 5 minutes or so until tender. Remove and place on a serving platter. Each person can rub a little umeboshi plum on the corn for garnish instead of butter.

Creamed Corn and Fresh Lima Beans

> 4 to 5 ears sweet corn, husks and silk removed
> 2 cups fresh lima beans, shells removed
> 1/2 cup water
> pinch sea salt

Take a box grater and finely grate the corn off the cobs. Place the corn, lima beans, water, and sea salt in a saucepan. Cover and bring to a boil. Reduce the flame to medium-low and simmer 10 minutes until tender and creamy. Place in a serving bowl.

Glazed Carrots

2 cups carrot, sliced in thin rounds or diagonals
1/2 cup water
3 Tbsp brown rice syrup or barley malt
several drops shoyu
1 Tbsp black sesame seeds, toasted

Place the carrot, syrup, and water in a pot. Add several drops of shoyu. Cover and bring to a boil. Reduce the flame to medium-low and simmer 5 to 7 minutes. Remove the cover, turn the flame to high, and cook off all remaining liquid. Place in a serving bowl. Garnish with toasted sesame seeds.

New England Boiled Dinner

This dish can be prepared in a heavy enameled cast iron pot or casserole dish that can also be used for serving.

2 lb cooked seitan
1 cup turnip, sliced in thick wedges
1 cup rutabaga, sliced in chunks
2 cups taro or albi potato, peeled, and halved or quartered
1 cup carrot, sliced in 2 inch long rounds
1/2 head green cabbage, sliced in 1 inch thick wedges
sesame oil, for braising seitan (optional)
shoyu
water

Place a small amount of oil in the pot and heat. Place the seitan chunks in the pot and brown on each side. Place the other vegetables in their own separate sections in the skillet so that they surround the seitan. Add water to half-cover. Add several drops shoyu for a mild flavor. Cover and bring to a boil. Reduce the flame to medium-low and simmer for 30 to 35 minutes until all vegetables are tender. Remove cover and transfer to the dining table.

Vegetable Nabe

The word "nabe" means "pot" in Japanese. It is essentially a method of cooking a variety of foods in one pot so as to create a complete meal. This method of cooking is called "nabemono," or "things cooking in one pot." Many types of pots can be used in nabemono cooking, such as clay pots called "donabe," cast iron pots called "tetsu-nabe," and brass pots called "hoko-nabe." A cast iron skillet may also be used for making "sukiyaki." Nabe is usually prepared at the table over a portable burner. It can also be prepared on the stove and transferred to the table if a portable burner is not available. Nabe is similar to fondue and Mongolian hot-pot cooking.

Plenty of vegetables are used in nabe, often with other ingredients such as fresh or deep-fried tofu, fish and shellfish, noodles, mochi (pounded rice taffy), tempeh (fermented soybeans), seitan (wheat gluten), and fu (puffed wheat gluten). A large nabe makes enough food for four people. Smaller nabe can be used for fewer people.

Summer Nabe

8 oz cooked udon, somen, or soba, rinsed and drained
3 shiitake mushrooms, soaked, stems removed, and
  sliced or quartered
1 inch piece kombu
2 cups Chinese cabbage, sliced in 1 inch squares
1 lb tofu, cubed
1/2 cup carrot, sliced in thin diagonals
1/2 cup squash, thinly sliced
1/2 cup daikon, sliced in thin half-moons
1/2 cup leek, sliced in 1/2 inch diagonals
1 cup bok choy or other dark greens, sliced in 1 inch
  pieces
1 cup water, for dip sauce
2 Tbsp shoyu, for dip sauce
1 tsp ginger juice or natural mustard, for dip sauce

water, for cooking vegetables, including shiitake and
kombu soaking water

Place the shiitake and kombu in the nabe. Add enough
water to half-fill the pot. Place the nabe over a medium flame,
cover, and bring to a boil. When the water is boiling, remove
the kombu and set aside for future use. Place all the cut vegetables and noodles on a big platter. Add all the ingredients to
the pot, keeping them in their own separate sections. Do not
mix. Cover and cook. Do not over-cook. Remove the vegetables and noodles from the pot as they are done and place in
the dip sauce before eating. You may keep adding more foods
to the pot to replenish as desired.

To prepare the dip sauce, place 1 cup of water in a saucepan. Add the shoyu and heat. Simmer 2 to 3 minutes. Add the
ginger juice or mustard, mix, and place in small dipping
bowls for each person.

Seafood Oden (Winter Nabe)

1 strip kombu, 1 inch by 2 inches after soaking
4 to 5 shiitake, soaked, stems removed, and quartered
8 to 10 rounds of daikon, 1/2 inch thick
1 lb tofu, sliced in 1/4 to 1/2 inch thick slices and deep-
   fried until golden
sesame oil, for deep-frying tofu (optional, you may use
   fresh tofu instead)
1 cup turnip, sliced in thick wedges
1 cup carrot, sliced in thick diagonals
1 cup small cooking onions or shallots, peeled
4 to 5 rounds of fu (dried wheat gluten), soaked and
   sliced in bite-sized pieces
1 lb boneless white meat fish, sliced in chunks (optional)
1 lb medium or large shrimp, pre-cooked
8 to 10 fresh oysters, removed from shells and rinsed
8 to 10 fresh clams, removed from shells and rinsed
4 cups Chinese cabbage, sliced in 1 inch pieces

6 to 8 cups water, including shiitake and kombu soaking water
1/4 cup mirin (sweet cooking sake; optional)
shoyu
water, for pre-cooking daikon rounds

Place the daikon in a saucepan and half-cover with water. Cover the pan and bring to a boil. Reduce the flame to
medium-low and simmer for 20 minutes. Remove and place
on a platter. Place a large nabe over a medium flame and add
the 6 to 8 cups water and the shiitake and kombu. Slowly
bring to a boil. Add shoyu for a mild salt taste. Add the mirin
if desired. Place the pre-cooked daikon in the pot. Add the fu,
deep-fried tofu, onion, carrot, and turnip. Cover and simmer
for about 1 hour or more until all ingredients are very tender.
Add the fish and shellfish. Cover and cook about 5 minutes.
Add the Chinese cabbage, cover, and simmer 1 to 2 minutes.
Remove the lid and place the nabe on the table under a pot
holder. Everyone can serve themselves from the pot.

Sukiyaki (Vegetable Skillet)

Sukiyaki can be prepared on the stove and transferred to the
dining table. You may use one large cast iron skillet or small
skillets for each person.

8 oz cooked udon, rinsed and drained
1 lb tofu, cubed
6 cups water
1 strip kombu, 1 inch by 2 inches after soaking
8 to 10 fresh shiitake, stems removed, halved or left
whole if small
8 to 10 slices cooked seitan, 1/4 to 1/2 inch thick
8 to 10 slices yellow summer squash, cut in 1/2 inch
thick diagonals
1/2 cup carrot, sliced in thin diagonals
1 cup mung bean sprouts, rinsed
2 bunches watercress, chopped

2 cups Chinese cabbage, sliced in 1 inch squares
shoyu

Place the water in a saucepan. Add the kombu and shii-take. Add enough shoyu for a very mild salt taste. Cover and bring to a boil. Reduce the flame to medium-low and simmer 10 minutes. Remove kombu and set aside for future use. Pour the liquid into a large cast iron skillet and bring to a boil. Place the udon, tofu, carrot, seitan, and summer squash in the skillet, keeping each separate. Cover, reduce the flame to medium-low, and simmer 2 to 3 minutes until the carrot and squash are tender. Add the Chinese cabbage, watercress, and bean sprouts. Cover and simmer 1 minute until tender but the greens are still brightly colored. Remove the cover and transfer the skillet to the dining table. Each person can help themselves. Dip sauce can be prepared if desired.

Yu Dofu (Quick Tofu and Vegetables)

This dish can be cooked in a nabe or an attractive stainless steel pot that can also be used for serving. Yu Dofu is normally unseasoned, but a mild dip sauce can be prepared if desired.

> **2 lb tofu, cubed**
> **2 cups Chinese cabbage, sliced in 1 inch thick pieces**
> **1 cup carrot, sliced in thin matchsticks**
> **8 to 10 fresh shiitake, stems removed**
> **6 cups water**

Place the water in a pot, cover, and bring to a boil. Add the shiitake and sliced carrot. Cover and simmer 2 to 3 minutes. Add the tofu, cover, and simmer 2 to 3 minutes. Add the Chinese cabbage, cover, and simmer 1 to 1 1/2 minutes. Remove the pot from the stove and transfer to the dining table. Each person can help themselves from the pot.

Yuki Nabe (Snow Nabe)

This traditional Buddhist vegetarian dish helps dissolve stagnation and relax inner tension.

1 medium-sized fresh daikon, peeled
1 lb tofu, cubed
small pinch sea salt

Finely grate the daikon and place in a nabe pot or small stainless steel saucepan. Add the sea salt. Cover and bring to a boil. Simmer 3 to 5 minutes. Remove the cover, mix the daikon with a wooden spoon, and place the tofu in the pot. Mix, cover, and simmer another 2 to 3 minutes. Ladle into serving bowls. You may garnish with chopped scallion or chives.

2
Pressed and Marinated Vegetables

Pressing is a form of quick-pickling. Vegetables are mixed with sea salt or natural vinegar and put under pressure. They begin to ferment and release energy. Pressed vegetables are often referred to as "pressed salad," and are more easily digestible than raw vegetables. Like quickly pickled vegetables, marinated vegetables are also slightly fermented. As a result, both methods generally produce upward, expansive effects.

Pressed Salad with Sea Salt

2 cups green cabbage, finely shredded
1/4 cup celery, sliced on a thin diagonal
1/2 cup red onion, sliced in thin half-rings
1/4 cup red apple, quartered and sliced thin
1 tsp sea salt

Place all vegetables in a mixing bowl. Add the sea salt and mix thoroughly with your hands. Place the vegetables in a pickle press and press for 2 to 2 1/2 hours. Remove and squeeze out excess salty liquid. Taste a piece of vegetable. If too salty, rinse quickly in a strainer under cold water. Squeeze again and place in a serving dish.

Pressed Salad with Sea Salt and Brown Rice Vinegar

2 cups Chinese cabbage, shredded
1/2 cup red onion, sliced in thin rings or half-rings
1/4 cup celery, sliced on a thin diagonal
1/4 cup red radish, sliced in thin rounds or half-moons
1/4 cup cucumber, sliced in thin half-moons
1/2 tsp sea salt
1 to 2 tsp brown rice vinegar

Mix the vegetables and sea salt and place in a pickle press. Press for 45 minutes to 1 hour or longer if desired. Squeeze out excess water and taste. If too salty, rinse quickly under cold water in a strainer. Place in a serving bowl. Add the brown rice vinegar and mix well. Serve.

Pressed Salad with Umeboshi Vinegar

1 cup red radish, sliced in thin rounds
1/2 cup radish greens, chopped fine
1 cup romaine or leafy lettuce, pulled apart in bite-sized pieces
1/4 cup onion, sliced in half-rings
1/4 cup celery, sliced on a thin diagonal
1/4 cup cucumber, sliced in thin quarters
2 tsp umeboshi vinegar

Mix the vegetables with the umeboshi vinegar. Place in a pickle press. Press for 45 minutes. Remove and squeeze out excess liquid. Taste and if too salty, rinse quickly under cold water in a strainer. Squeeze again and place in a serving bowl.

Pressed Red Radish

 2 cups red radish, sliced in thin rounds
 1/2 tsp sea salt
 2 tsp mirin (optional)
 1 tsp sweet brown rice or brown rice vinegar
 3 Tbsp black sesame seeds, roasted

Mix the sliced radish, sea salt, mirin, and vinegar. Place in a pickle press and press for 1 hour or so. Remove, squeeze out liquid, and taste. If too salty, rinse in a strainer. Squeeze again and place in a serving dish. Toss in the roasted sesame seeds and serve.

Red and Green Coleslaw

 1 cup red cabbage, shredded
 1 cup green cabbage, shredded
 1/4 cup celery, sliced on a thin diagonal
 1/2 cup onion, sliced in thin half-rings
 1 tsp sea salt
 1/4 cup natural tofu mayonnaise (optional)

Mix the vegetables and sea salt. Place in a pickle press and press for 2 hours. Remove, squeeze out liquid, and taste. If too salty, rinse and squeeze again. Place in a mixing bowl and mix in the tofu mayonnaise. Place in a serving bowl.

Waldorf Salad

 3 1/2 cups green cabbage, very finely shredded
 1/4 cup carrot, coarsely grated
 1/2 cup walnuts, roasted and chopped
 1/4 cup celery, sliced on a thin diagonal
 1 cup red apple, cut in 1/4 inch thick chunks
 1/4 cup raisins

1/4 cup seedless red grapes

Place all ingredients in a mixing bowl and mix thoroughly. Serve with the following **Green Goddess Dressing**:

2 to 3 umeboshi plums, pits removed
1 cup water
2 Tbsp onion, grated
3/4 cup cooked brown rice
1/2 cup parsley, finely minced
2 Tbsp tahini
1 Tbsp shoyu

Place all ingredients in a blender and blend until smooth and creamy or grind in a suribachi until smooth and creamy. Mix the dressing in with the Waldorf Salad ingredients.

Brown rice or sweet brown rice vinegar can be added for a sweeter flavor. You can also add a little natural mustard or horseradish for a slightly pungent flavor.

Marinated Lotus Root Salad

2 cups fresh lotus root, halved or quartered and sliced
   very thin
2 Tbsp shoyu
2 Tbsp brown rice vinegar
2 Tbsp water
2 Tbsp mirin
2 tsp tan sesame seeds, roasted
1 Tbsp scallion, chopped very fine
1 to 2 drops fresh ginger juice

Mix all ingredients in a mixing bowl and let sit for 30 minutes to 1 hour. Remove, drain, and place in a serving bowl.

Marinated Daikon and Carrot Salad

1 cup daikon, sliced in very thin matchsticks
1 cup carrot, sliced in very thin matchsticks
1/4 cup raisins, boiled 2 minutes
1 tsp white miso
1 tsp mirin
1 tsp shoyu
1/4 tsp fresh ginger juice
1 Tbsp water
1/4 cup parsley, minced

Place the miso, mirin, shoyu, ginger juice, and water in a suribachi and purée. Add the daikon, carrot, and raisins. Let sit for 30 minutes to 1 hour. Remove, drain, and place in a serving dish. Garnish with parsley and serve.

Tofu Stuffed Cucumbers

1 lb firm style tofu
1 tsp umeboshi paste
2 Tbsp onion, finely grated
1 Tbsp scallion or chives, finely chopped
2 Tbsp roasted tahini
1/2 tsp shoyu
2 cucumbers

Place umeboshi paste, onion, scallion or chives, and tahini in a suribachi and purée until smooth and creamy. Place a hand food mill on top of the suribachi and purée the tofu through it into the suribachi. Purée all ingredients together. Remove the ends from the cucumber and hollow out the center by removing the seeds with a melon baller. Stuff the cucumbers with the tofu mixture, packing it in firmly with a wooden pestle or spoon.

Slice each cucumber in half. Slice each half in half. Then slice each quarter in half. You should now have 16 stuffed cucumber slices. Place on a serving bowl. As a variation, try stuffing the cucumbers with homemade, miso-pickled tofu cheese and chives or scallion.

Puréed Squash Aspic

> 3 cups water or kombu stock
> 5 to 6 Tbsp agar flakes
> pinch of sea salt
> 4 cups buttercup squash or Hokkaido pumpkin, skin
>   removed and sliced in small cubes
> 1 Tbsp parsley, minced, for garnish

Place the the water, agar flakes, squash chunks, and sea salt in a pot. Bring to a boil, stirring occasionally. Reduce the flame to medium-low and simmer until the squash is tender, about 5 minutes. Purée the squash and all liquid through a hand food mill into a bowl. Pour into a shallow casserole or glass baking dish. Let sit in a cool place or refrigerate until jelled. Garnish with chopped parsley. Slice and serve. Cauliflower, carrot, broccoli, and other sweet vegetables can be used instead of squash.

Cabbage and Carrot Aspic

> 4 to 5 cup kombu stock
> 5 to 6 Tbsp agar flakes
> pinch of sea salt
> 1/2 cup raisins, soaked 10 minutes
> 1 cup apple, sliced in cubes
> 1 cup carrot, coarsely grated and blanched 1 minute
> 1 cup green cabbage, finely shredded

Place the stock, agar flakes, and sea salt in a pot and bring to a boil. Reduce the flame to medium-low and simmer 3 minutes. Place the raisins in the bottom of a casserole or glass baking dish. Layer the carrot and cabbage on top. Slowly pour the hot liquid over the raisins and vegetables. Place in a cool place or refrigerate until jelled. Slice and serve with the following **Miso-Apple Dressing**:

2 Tbsp grated apple
1 1/2 Tbsp barley miso
1 tsp roasted tahini
1/2 cup water

Place the water and miso in a saucepan and heat. Turn the flame off and allow to cool. Add the grated apple and tahini. Place in a suribachi and purée. Place in a serving dish. Cut the aspic in squares and serve a spoonful of sauce over each slice.

3
Sautéed and Stir-Fried Vegetables

Quick-sautéing and stir-frying utilize strong heat and energy and accelerate the actively expanding energy in vegetables and other foods. You can sauté with or without oil, depending on your individual needs. Sautéing for a longer time, as we do in the dish known as *Kinpira*, makes vegetables have more concentrated and strengthening effects.

Quick Sautéed Greens

2 cups dark leafy greens (any variety), stems removed
several drops sesame oil
several drops shoyu

Chop the stems of the greens into small pieces. Place them on a plate, keeping them separate from the leafy portion. Chop the leafy portion into 1 inch squares. Heat the oil in a skillet, add the stems, and sauté 1 minute. Add the leafy part and several drops of shoyu. Mix thoroughly with chopsticks or a wooden spoon and sauté for 2 to 3 minutes. The greens should be tender but still bright green in color. Remove and place in a serving dish.

Water Sautéed Greens

2 cups dark leafy greens, chopped in 1 inch squares
water
shoyu

Place enough water in a skillet to barely cover the bottom. Bring to a boil. Add the tougher stems first and sauté 1 minute. Add the leafy greens and several drops of shoyu. Sauté 2 to 3 minutes until tender but still bright green. Place in a serving dish.

Kinpira (Sautéed Carrot and Burdock)

Kinpira is a cooking style used in Japan for root and round-shaped vegetables. It is a combination of either oil- or water-sautéing and boiling. At the end of cooking the liquid is boiled off. The vegetables are cut in thin pieces so the dish cooks more quickly.

1 cup burdock, washed and sliced in thin matchsticks
1 cup carrot, washed and sliced in thin matchsticks
1/2 tsp fresh ginger juice
sesame oil
water
shoyu

Place 3 or 4 drops of oil in a cast iron or heavy skillet and heat. Add the burdock and sauté for 2 to 3 minutes. Add enough cold water to the skillet to almost cover the burdock. Layer the carrot on top of the burdock. Do not mix. Cover the skillet and bring the water to a boil. Reduce the flame to medium-low and cook about 7 to 10 minutes until the burdock is tender. (Wild burdock that you dig yourself will take a little longer to cook than burdock purchased at a natural food store, as it is tougher.) When the burdock is tender, sprinkle with several drops of shoyu for a mild salty flavor, cover, and cook for another 5 minutes or so. Remove the lid, turn the flame to high, and cook off most of the remaining liquid. When there is just a little liquid remaining in the bottom of the skillet, mix the carrot and burdock and add the ginger juice. Cook off all remaining liquid. Place in a serving dish.

Other vegetable combinations that can be used instead of carrot and burdock are: half-moon onion and matchstick carrot, matchstick carrot and parsnip, matchstick carrot and rutabaga or turnip, matchstick carrot and quartered and thinly sliced fresh lotus root, lotus root, and carrot, burdock, and dried tofu strips.

Water Sautéed Kinpira Burdock and Carrot

1 cup burdock, sliced in thin matchsticks
1 cup carrot, sliced in thin matchsticks
water
shoyu
2 tsp roasted tan or black sesame seeds (optional)

Place enough water in a heavy skillet to just barely cover the bottom. Bring to a boil over a high flame. Add the burdock and sauté for 2 to 3 minutes, as if there were oil in the skillet. Add enough cold water to almost cover the burdock. Layer the carrot on top of the burdock. Cover the skillet and bring to a boil. Reduce the flame to medium-low and simmer for 7 to 10 minutes until the burdock is tender. Add several drops of shoyu, cover, and simmer another 5 minutes. Remove the cover, turn the flame to high, and cook off most of the remaining liquid. Mix the carrot and burdock, add the sesame seeds, and cook off all remaining liquid. Place in a serving dish.

If you like a slightly spicy taste, add 1/2 teaspoon ginger juice when you add the sesame seeds.

Sautéed Squash and Onions

1 1/2 cups buttercup or butternut squash, seeds removed and sliced thin
1/2 cup onion, sliced in thin half-moons
sesame oil (optional)
1/4 cup water
shoyu

Place 3 to 4 drops sesame oil in a skillet and heat. Sauté the onion for 2 to 3 minutes. Add the squash and water. Cover the skillet and bring water to a boil. Reduce the flame to medium-low, add several drops of shoyu, and simmer for 5 to 7 minutes until the squash is tender. Remove the cover and cook off any remaining liquid. Place in a serving dish.

Sautéed Mushrooms and Garlic

3 cups organic mushrooms, sliced thin
2 to 3 cloves garlic, minced (optional)
sesame or extra virgin olive oil
shoyu
2 Tbsp chives, finely chopped

Place the oil in a skillet and add the garlic. Heat oil and sauté the garlic for 1 minute. Add the mushrooms and several drops of shoyu. Cover and cook over a medium-low flame for 3 to 5 minutes. Remove the cover, mix in the chives, and cook off any remaining liquid. Place in a serving dish.

Pan-Fried Parsnip

3 cups parsnip, cut into matchsticks or shaved
1 tsp dark or light sesame oil
shoyu
several drops of water

Heat the oil and sauté the parsnips for 3 to 4 minutes. Add several drops of shoyu and water. Cover and reduce the flame to medium-low. Sauté for another 7 to 10 minutes until tender and slightly browned. Place in a serving bowl.

Green Beans Almondine

> 3 cups green string beans, stems removed and cut
>   French style or on a long thin diagonal
> 1/2 cup roasted almonds, slivered
> shoyu
> 1/4 cup water
> sesame oil

Place several drops of sesame oil in a skillet and heat. Add the string beans and sauté for 2 to 3 minutes. Add 1/4 cup water, cover, and bring to a boil. Reduce the flame to medium-low and simmer for 5 to 7 minutes. Remove the cover and add several drops of shoyu and the slivered almonds. Sauté, without a cover, for another 2 to 3 minutes. Place in a serving dish.

Cabbage and Sauerkraut Stir-Fry

> 2 1/2 cups green cabbage, shredded
> 1/2 cup sauerkraut
> shoyu
> sesame oil

Heat several drops of sesame oil in a skillet. Sauté the cabbage and sauerkraut for 4 to 5 minutes by stirring constantly with chopsticks or a wooden spoon. Add several drops of shoyu and sauté another 3 to 4 minutes. Place in a serving bowl.

Chinese Cabbage Stir-Fry

3 cups Chinese cabbage, sliced in 1 inch squares
sesame oil
shoyu

Heat several drops of sesame oil in a skillet. Sauté the cabbage for 3 to 4 minutes. Add several drops of shoyu and sauté 2 to 3 minutes. Place in a serving bowl.

Sautéed Glazed Baby Carrots

3 cups baby carrots
corn oil
1/2 cup water
2 tsp brown rice syrup
shoyu

Heat several drops of corn oil in a skillet. Add the carrots and sauté for 3 to 4 minutes. Add the water and rice syrup. Cover and bring to a boil. Reduce the flame to medium-low and simmer for 2 to 3 minutes. Add several drops of shoyu, cover, and simmer another 3 to 4 minutes. Remove the cover, turn the flame to high, and cook off all remaining liquid while stirring constantly. Place in a serving bowl.

Corn Meal-Fried Summer Squash or Zucchini

1 cup corn meal
1/4 tsp sea salt
3 cups summer squash or zucchini, sliced in 1/2 inch
  thick rounds
corn or sesame oil
shoyu
1/4 cup grated daikon

Mix the corn meal and sea salt in a mixing bowl. Place the summer squash or zucchini in the bowl and mix to evenly coat all pieces with the corn meal mixture. Place enough corn or sesame oil in a skillet to cover the bottom. Heat the oil. Place the sliced summer squash or zucchini in the skillet. Place 2 to 3 drops of shoyu on each piece of squash. Cover the skillet and cook for 3 to 4 minutes until golden brown. Flip the slices over and fry the other side as above. Repeat until all slices have been fried. Place on a serving platter. Serve with a little grated daikon as a garnish.

Sautéed Pepper With Miso

1 1/2 cups red bell pepper, seeds removed and sliced
1 1/2 cups green bell pepper, seeds removed and sliced
1/2 cup onion, sliced in thin half-moons
2 to 3 tsp barley or brown rice miso, puréed
1/2 cup water
sesame oil

Heat several drops of sesame oil in a skillet. Sauté the onion for 2 to 3 minutes. Add the pepper and sauté another 3 to 4 minutes. Add the miso and water. Cover and simmer over a medium-low flame for 7 to 10 minutes. Remove the cover, mix, and sauté 1 to 2 minutes longer. Place in a serving dish.

Stir-Fried Portabello Mushroom and Broccoli Rabé

1 portabello mushroom, sliced
2 cups broccoli rabé (Italian broccoli), chopped in 1 to 2 inch lengths
1/4 cup water
2 cloves garlic, minced (optional)
sesame or extra-virgin olive oil
shoyu

Place several drops oil in a skillet. Add the garlic and heat. Sauté the garlic for 1 minute. Add the mushroom and sauté 2 to 3 minutes. Add the broccoli rabe, water, and several drops of shoyu. Cover and bring to a boil. Reduce the flame to medium-low and simmer 2 minutes. Remove the cover, turn the flame to high, and cook off the remaining liquid, stirring constantly. Place in a serving bowl.

Cauliflower in Creamy White Sauce

> 1 medium cauliflower, sliced in florets (about 3 cups)
> 1 Tbsp corn oil
> 2 cups water
> 1/3 to 1/2 cup unbleached white or brown rice flour
> sea salt
> 1 Tbsp chives, scallion, or parsley, finely chopped

Heat the oil in a skillet. Sauté the cauliflower for 2 to 3 minutes. Add the flour and sauté 1 to 2 minutes until the cauliflower is completely coated with the flour. Gradually add the water to the skillet, stirring constantly to prevent lumping. Continue stirring until the sauce becomes thick. Add enough sea salt for a mild salt flavor. Cover, reduce the flame to medium-low, and simmer for 7 to 10 minutes until the cauliflower is tender. Place in a serving bowl and garnish with chopped chives, scallion, or parsley.

Variations can be created by using different combinations of vegetables such as peas, carrot, broccoli, mushroom, and onion.

Sautéed Onion and Seitan in Mustard Sauce

> 1 Spanish or large onion, sliced in 1/4 inch thick rounds
> 1 lb seitan, sliced in thin slices or strips
> 1/4 cup seitan cooking liquid
> 1/4 cup water
> 2 tsp natural mustard

several drops shoyu
2 Tbsp scallion, finely sliced, for garnish
sesame oil

Heat several drops of sesame oil in a skillet. Add the onion and sauté for 2 to 3 minutes. Mix the mustard, seitan cooking liquid, and water, and pour over the onion. Lay the seitan on top of the onion. Cover and bring to a boil. Reduce the flame to medium-low and simmer for 5 to 7 minutes until the onion is tender and the seitan is hot. If needed, add several drops of shoyu for extra flavor, cover, and cook another 2 to 3 minutes. Remove the cover, add the scallion, mix, and cook another 2 minutes. Place in a serving dish. Sliced tempeh may be substituted for seitan in this dish.

Stir-Fried Chinese Vegetables in Kuzu Sauce

1/2 cup onion, sliced in thin half-moons
1 cup Chinese cabbage, sliced in 1 inch squares
1/2 cup bok choy, sliced in 1 inch squares
1/2 cup snow peas, stems removed
1/2 cup fresh shiitake mushrooms, stems removed and sliced thin
1/2 cup tofu, cubed
1/2 cup mung bean sprouts
1/2 tsp sesame oil
shoyu
1/2 tsp fresh ginger juice
1 cup water
1 tsp kuzu, diluted in 2 tsp water

Heat the oil in a skillet or wok. Sauté the onion for 1 minute. Add the carrot and shiitake mushroom and sauté 1 to 2 minutes. Add the Chinese cabbage, bok choy, tofu, snow peas, and mung bean sprouts. Sauté 1 minute. Add water and bring to a boil. Add the diluted kuzu, stirring constantly to prevent lumping. Season to taste with several drops of shoyu. Simmer 1 to 2 minutes. Add the ginger juice, mix, and cook 1 minute. Place in a serving bowl. These vegetables can be served as a side dish or over cooked rice or noodles.

Stir-Fried Savoy Cabbage with Black Sesame Seeds

> 3 cups savoy cabbage, shredded
> pinch of sea salt
> sesame oil
> 1 tsp toasted black sesame seeds, for garnish

Heat several drops sesame oil in a skillet. Add the cabbage and sea salt. Stir-fry for 3 to 4 minutes until slightly crisp and brightly colored. Mix in the toasted sesame seeds. Place in a serving dish.

Scrambled Tofu and Vegetables

> 1 lb firm style tofu
> 1/2 cup onion, diced
> 1/4 cup carrot, diced
> 1/2 cup mushroom, sliced thin
> 1/4 cup red pepper, diced (you may substitute red radish rounds)
> 1/4 cup green pepper, diced (you may substitute chopped scallion)
> 1/4 cup sweet corn, removed from cob
> 1/2 tsp sesame oil (optional; you may water sauté)
> shoyu or umeboshi vinegar

Heat the oil in a skillet. Add the onion and sauté 1 to 2 minutes. Layer the other ingredients in the following order: carrot, mushroom, pepper, and sweet corn. With your hands crumble the tofu over the vegetables. Cover the skillet and reduce the flame to medium-low. Cook until the tofu is fluffy and the vegetables are almost done. Add several drops of shoyu or umeboshi vinegar. Cover and simmer another 3 to 5 minutes. Remove the cover, turn the flame to high, and cook off most of the liquid. Place in a serving dish.

Sautéed Brussel Sprouts and Walnuts

> 3 cups Brussel sprouts, stems removed and sliced in half
> 1/2 cup roasted walnuts, coarsely chopped (you may substitute pumpkin seeds, sunflower seeds, pecans, or chopped almonds)
> sesame oil
> 1/4 cup water
> shoyu

Heat several drops of sesame oil in a skillet. Add the Brussel sprouts and sauté for 1 to 2 minutes. Add the water and several drops of shoyu. Cover and bring to a boil. Reduce the flame to medium-low and simmer for 2 to 3 minutes until tender. Add the walnuts and simmer until all liquid is gone. Place in a serving bowl.

Sweet and Sour Tofu and Vegetables

> 2 cups tofu, cubed
> 1 cup broccoli, sliced in florets
> 1/2 cup cauliflower, sliced in florets
> 1/4 cup carrot, sliced in thin diagonals
> 1/2 cup onion, sliced in half-moons
> 1/4 cup celery, sliced in thin diagonals
> 1/4 cup fresh shiitake, stems removed and sliced
> sesame oil
> 3 cups water
> shoyu, to taste
> brown rice vinegar, to taste
> 4 Tbsp kuzu, diluted in 5 Tbsp water
> 1/2 cup brown rice syrup

Heat several drops of sesame oil. Sauté the onion for 1 to 2 minutes. Add the shiitake and celery and sauté 1 to 2 minutes. Add the cauliflower and carrot. Add the water, cover, and bring to a boil. Reduce the flame to medium-low and simmer 1 minute. Add the broccoli, cover, and simmer 1 minute. Add the kuzu, stirring constantly to prevent lumping, until thick and translucent. Place the brown rice syrup in the pot and mix. Add a small amount of brown rice vinegar for a mild sweet and sour flavor. Add several drops of shoyu for a mild salt flavor. Place the tofu and snow peas in the pot, cover, and simmer another 2 minutes. Remove and place in a serving bowl.

This dish may be served as a side dish over cooked rice or noodles. You may substitute cooked seitan chunks for tofu cubes.

Sautéed Lotus Root

> 2 cups fresh lotus root, sliced in thin rounds or half-moons
> 1 cup onion, sliced in thin half-moons
> sesame oil
> shoyu
> 1/4 cup water
> 1/2 tsp fresh ginger juice

Heat several drops of sesame oil in a skillet. Sauté the onion for 1 to 2 minutes. Add enough water to almost cover the onion. Layer the lotus root on top of the onion. Cover and bring to a boil. Reduce the flame to medium-low and simmer 3 to 5 minutes. Add several drops of shoyu, cover, and simmer another 3 to 4 minutes. Remove the cover, turn the flame to high, and add the ginger juice. Mix thoroughly until all liquid is gone. Place in a serving bowl.

4
Deep-Fried Vegetables

Deep-frying utilizes very intense heat and energy. Vegetable oil is the agent used to convey intense heat to vegetables and other foods. The oil is in turn balanced by salt, usually in the form of shoyu. Because of the high volume of salt and oil used in this method of cooking, we use it only on special occasions. Deep-fried vegetables are best consumed with garnishes, such as grated daikon, that help in the digestion of oil.

Deep-Fried Vegetable Chips

1/2 cup fresh lotus root, sliced in thin rounds
1/2 cup parsnip, sliced in thin diagonals
1/2 cup carrot, sliced in thin diagonals
1/2 cup rutabaga, sliced in thin quarters
light sesame, sunflower, or safflower oil, for deep frying
1/2 cup water, for dip sauce
2 to 3 tsp shoyu, for dip sauce
1/2 tsp fresh ginger juice, for dip sauce

Heat 2 to 3 inches of oil in a deep-frying pot. Deep-fry the lotus root until golden and crispy. Remove, place on paper towels, and drain. Repeat until all vegetables have been deep-fried until golden and drained. To prepare the dip sauce, place the water and shoyu in a saucepan. Bring to a boil. Reduce the flame to medium-low and simmer 3 to 4 minutes. Turn off and add the ginger juice. Mix the ginger in. Place in a small bowl. Dip the vegetable chips in the dip sauce before eating. For variety, try adding 1 teaspoon prepared mustard or 1 tablespoon grated ginger (instead of ginger juice) in the dip sauce.

Deep-Fried Squash Balls

4 cups buttercup squash or Hokkaido pumpkin, seeds and green skin removed and cut in chunks
water, for cooking squash
pinch of sea salt, for cooking squash
1/2 cup onion, minced
1/2 cup sweet corn, removed from cob
2 tsp parsley or chives, finely chopped
1/2 to 1 cup whole wheat pastry flour
2 cups very fine bread crumbs or corn meal
1/2 cup grated daikon, for garnish
shoyu, for daikon garnish
1 Tbsp scallion, chopped, for garnish
sesame, sunflower, or safflower oil, for deep-frying

Place the squash chunks in a pot. Add enough water to half-cover the chunks. Add the sea salt, cover, and bring to a boil. Reduce the flame to medium-low and simmer 5 minutes or until tender. Purée the squash through a hand food mill, adding the squash cooking water if needed. The purée should be rather thick, not soupy. Place the purée in a mixing bowl and add the onion, sweet corn, and parsley or chives. Mix thoroughly. If needed, gradually add the whole wheat pastry flour until the purée is thick and can easily be rolled into small balls the size of a golf ball. Roll all of the purée into balls. Then roll all of the balls in the bread crumbs, completely coating them. Place on a platter.

Heat 2 to 3 inches of oil in a heavy deep-frying pot. When hot, place 5 to 7 balls in the hot oil and deep-fry until golden and crisp. Remove and drain on paper towels. Repeat until all balls have been deep-fried and drained. Place on a serving platter.

To prepare the daikon garnish, place finely grated daikon in a small bowl, and add the scallion and several drops of shoyu. Serve each person 2 tablespoons of daikon garnish to be eaten along with the squash balls.

Deep-Fried Squash and Chestnut Balls

14 to 16 dried chestnuts
2 to 2 1/2 cups water, for cooking chestnuts
pinch of sea salt, for cooking chestnuts
4 cups squash purée (as per above recipe but without other vegetables)
1/2 to 1 cup pastry flour
1 to 2 cups very fine bread crumbs
light sesame, sunflower, or safflower oil, for deep-frying

Place the chestnuts in a pressure cooker. Add the water and sea salt. Cover and bring up to pressure. Reduce the flame to medium-low and cook for 40 to 45 minutes. Remove from the flame and let the pressure come down. Remove the chestnuts and place in a bowl or on a plate.

Place the squash purée in a mixing bowl. Add enough flour to make a very thick purée that will hold together when rolled into balls just slightly bigger than golf balls. After you roll the purée into balls, insert a cooked chestnut into the center of each ball, making sure the chestnut is completely covered by purée. Roll the balls in bread crumbs.

Heat 2 to 3 inches of oil in a heavy deep-frying pot. When hot, deep-fry 5 to 7 balls at a time until golden and crisp. Remove and drain on paper towels. Repeat until all balls are deep-fried and drained. Place on a serving platter.

Deep-Fried Corn Fritters

1 cup sweet corn, removed from the cob
1/2 cup whole wheat pastry flour
1/2 cup corn flour
1/2 cup brown rice mochi, coarsely grated
1/2 cup mushroom, diced
1/4 cup onion, diced
1/4 cup parsley, minced
1/8 tsp sea salt
3/4 cup water
1 tsp kuzu, diluted in 2 tsp water
light sesame, sunflower, or safflower oil, for deep-
    frying

Heat 2 to 3 inches of oil in a heavy deep-frying pot. While the oil is heating up, place the flour, grated mochi, vegetables, and sea salt in a mixing bowl. Mix thoroughly. Add the water and diluted kuzu. Mix thoroughly again.

When the oil is hot, take a tablespoon of batter and drop it into the oil. Repeat, placing about 5 tablespoons of batter in the hot oil. Deep-fry until all batter is golden and crisp. Remove and drain on paper towels. Repeat until all batter has been deep-fried and drained. Place on a serving platter. Serve with shoyu-ginger dip sauce or grated daikon garnish as in the above recipes.

Deep-Fried Fish and Vegetable Balls

1/2 lb cod, haddock, scrod, sole, or other white meat
    fish (without skin or bones), washed
1/4 cup unbleached white or whole wheat flour
1 tsp sea salt
3 Tbsp mirin (optional), if not using increase the
    amount of water 3 by Tbsp
2 scallions, sliced thin
4 Tbsp carrot, minced
4 Tbsp celery, minced

2 tsp black sesame seeds, washed
2 Tbsp kuzu, diluted in 2 Tbsp water
1/2 cup whole wheat flour, to roll fish balls in
light sesame, sunflower, or safflower oil, for deep-
   frying

Cut the fish into small pieces and purée in a blender, adding a little at a time until you have a thick paste. Remove and place in a mixing bowl. Add the unbleached white flour, sea salt, mirin, vegetables, and sesame seeds. Mix thoroughly. Add the diluted kuzu to the mixture. Mix all ingredients until you have a smooth paste.

Place the 1/2 cup whole wheat flour in a bowl. Form the fish paste into 14 to 16 small balls about the size of a golf ball. Roll each ball in the flour, evenly coating them. Deep-fry in 2 to 3 inches of hot oil until golden brown and crisp. Remove and drain on paper towels.

Seitan and Vegetable Balls

1 1/2 lb cooked seitan, finely chopped
1/2 cup onion, finely minced
1/4 cup mushroom, minced
1/4 cup green pepper, finely minced
1 cup whole wheat bread cubes
1 Tbsp kuzu, diluted in 2 Tbsp water
light sesame, sunflower, or safflower oil, for deep-
   frying

Place the seitan in a hand food mill and grind into a mixing bowl. Add the vegetables, bread cubes, and kuzu. Mix thoroughly with your hands. Form the mixture into 12 to 14 balls about the size of a golf ball, packing firmly so they hold together well.

Heat 2 to 3 inches of oil in a heavy deep-frying pot. When hot, place half the balls in the hot oil and deep-fry until golden and crisp. Remove and place on paper towels to drain. Repeat until all balls have been deep-fried and drained. Place on a serving platter or serve with spaghetti and carrot-beet sauce.

Tempeh-Vegetable Balls

    1 1/2 lb tempeh, boiled 10 minutes in plain water
    1/2 cup onion, minced
    1/4 cup sauerkraut, chopped fine
    1/4 cup celery, minced
    1/4 cup carrot, finely grated
    2 tsp natural mustard
    2 tsp shoyu
    1/4 to 1/2 cup whole wheat pastry flour
    small amount of water, if necessary
    light sesame, sunflower, or safflower oil, for deep-
      frying

After cooking the tempeh, break it into small pieces with your hands and place in a mixing bowl. Add the vegetables, sauerkraut, mustard, and shoyu, and gradually add the flour and a little bit of water. Mix thoroughly with your hands, squeezing the mixture through you fingers. Form the mixture into 12 to 14 balls about the size of a golf ball, packing firmly so they hold together.

Deep-fry until golden brown. Remove and drain on paper towels. Place on a serving platter.

Tofu-Vegetable Balls

    1 1/2 lb firm style tofu, drained and puréed in a hand
      food mill
    1/4 cup onion, minced
    1/4 cup celery, minced
    1/4 cup carrot, minced
    2 tsp black sesame seeds, roasted
    2 tsp green nori flakes (Ao nori)
    2 tsp shoyu or umeboshi vinegar

1/2 to 1 cup whole wheat pastry flour
1 tsp fresh ginger juice
light sesame, sunflower, or safflower oil, for deep-
  frying

Place the tofu purée in a mixing bowl. Add the vegetables, seeds, nori flakes, shoyu or umeboshi vinegar, and mix well. Add the ginger juice and gradually the flour until thick and smooth. Form into 12 to 14 golf ball-sized balls and deep-fry until golden brown and crisp. Drain and place on a serving platter.

Tofu-Vegetable Spring Rolls

1 lb firm style tofu, drained
1 cup mung bean sprouts
1/4 cup onion, diced
1/4 cup carrot, diced
1/4 cup mushroom, diced
2 tsp shoyu
12 to 14 natural spring roll wrappers
light sesame, sunflower, or safflower oil, for deep-
  frying
1/2 cup water, for dip sauce
2 to 3 tsp shoyu, for dip sauce
2 tsp natural mustard, for dip sauce
2 tsp scallion, finely chopped, for dip sauce

Use your hands to finely crumble the tofu into a mixing bowl. Add the vegetables and 2 teaspoonfuls of shoyu. Place about 1/4 cup of the tofu mixture in each spring roll wrapper and roll up. Heat about 1/4 inch of oil in a heavy skillet. Place half of the rolls in the skillet and fry until golden brown. Flip over and fry the other side until golden brown. Repeat until all rolls are fried. Drain and place on a serving platter.

To prepare the dip sauce, place the water, shoyu, and mustard in a saucepan and bring to a boil. Reduce the flame to low and simmer 2 to 3 minutes. Turn off and add the chopped scallion. Place the sauce in individual dipping bowls. Dip the rolls into the sauce when eating.

Deep-Fried Lotus Root Dumplings

> 2 cups fresh lotus root, finely grated
> 1/4 cup onion, minced
> 1/4 cup parsley or chives, minced
> whole wheat pastry flour
> pinch of sea salt
> light sesame, sunflower, or safflower oil, for deep-frying
> 1/2 cup water, for dip sauce
> 2 to 3 tsp shoyu, for dip sauce
> 1 tsp lemon juice, for dip sauce

Place the lotus root, onion, parsley or chives, and pinch of salt in a mixing bowl. Mix thoroughly. Add enough pastry flour to the mixture to form a thick paste that will hold together when formed into balls. Form the mixture into several balls the size of a golf ball and place on a plate. Heat 2 to 3 inches of water in a heavy deep-frying pot and deep-fry several balls at a time until golden and crisp. Remove and drain on paper towels. Repeat until all balls have been deep-fried.

To prepare the dip sauce, place the water and shoyu in a saucepan and heat. Simmer 3 to 4 minutes. Turn off the flame and add the lemon juice. Place the sauce in small individual dipping bowls. When eating, dip the balls into the dip sauce.

Aveline Kushi's Deep-Fried Stuffed Lotus Root

> 2 fresh pieces of lotus root, 4 to 5 inches long
> water, for boiling lotus root
> 4 Tbsp tahini
> 2 Tbsp barley or brown rice miso

1 tsp grated ginger
4 tsp parsley, minced

Deep Frying Batter

1 cup whole wheat pastry flour
1 tsp kuzu, diluted in 2 tsp water
1/8 tsp sea salt
2/3 to 3/4 cup water
light sesame, sunflower, or safflower oil
1/2 cup daikon, finely grated, for garnish

Wash the lotus root and place in a pot. Add water to half-cover. Cover the pot and bring to a boil. Reduce the flame to medium-low and simmer about 10 to 15 minutes until tender. Remove from the pot and cut off the ends of the lotus root.

Mix the miso, tahini, ginger, and parsley in a small mixing bowl. Gently pound one end of each lotus root into the miso mixture. This will force the mixture up into the hollow lotus chambers, filling the roots. Place the two stuffed roots in a dish or on a plate and let sit for about 1 hour, allowing the miso to draw out a little water from the lotus.

To prepare the batter, place the pastry flour and sea salt in a mixing bowl and mix well. Add the diluted kuzu and gradually add the water, mixing thoroughly. Roll the lotus in whole wheat flour, completely coating it.

Heat 2 to 3 inches of oil. When hot, dip the lotus root in the batter and then place in the hot oil. Deep-fry several minutes until golden and crisp on the outside. Remove and drain on paper towels. When the roots have cooled, cut them into 1/4 to 1/2 inch thick rounds and place them chambers facing up on a serving platter. Serve with a little grated daikon as a garnish.

Tempura

Vegetables and other foods which are dipped into batter and deep-fried until golden and crisp are known as *tempura*. Tempura is best when made with high quality vegetable oil and very fresh vegetables. The best type of pot for deep-frying is a heavy cast iron Dutch oven or deep skillet, although a heavy stainless steel pot will also do. Thin pots tend not to hold heat as well as heavier pots, thus when you place vegetables in the pot, the temperature lowers, producing a less crisp and sometimes soggy tempura. The temperature of the oil needs to remain fairly constant at all times, between 350 to 375 degrees F. If you do not have a thermometer, heat the oil and drop a morsel of batter into it. If the morsel stays on the bottom, the oil is not hot enough. If the morsel hits the bottom and comes up fairly quickly, it is hot enough. If the oil smokes, it is too hot and should be discarded. Start again with fresh oil.

There are two basic ways to tempura vegetables: for larger pieces of vegetables or whole leaves such as kale or parsley, whole string beans, mushrooms, or watercress, dip the vegetables into the batter and deep-fry. When using small cuts of vegetables such as matchsticks, half-moons, or diced vegetables, they can be mixed in the batter and then spooned into the hot oil. When the tempura is golden brown and crisp it is done.

Tempura Batter 1

1/2 cup whole wheat pastry flour
1/2 cup corn flour
1/8 to 1/4 tsp sea salt
1 to 1 1/2 Tbsp kuzu, diluted
3/4 to 1 cup cold water

Tempura Batter 2

1/2 cup whole wheat pastry flour
1/2 cup brown rice flour
1/8 to 1/4 tsp sea salt

1 to 1 1/2 Tbsp kuzu, diluted
3/4 to 1 cup cold water or plain sparkling water

Tempura Batter 3

1/2 cup whole wheat pastry flour
1/2 cup unbleached white flour
1/8 to 1/4 tsp sea salt
1 to 1 1/2 Tbsp kuzu, diluted
3/4 to 1 cup plain or sparkling water

Mix the dry ingredients in a mixing bowl. Add the kuzu and water. Chill the batter, after mixing thoroughly, in the refrigerator for 1/2 hour or so. Dip sliced vegetables in the batter and deep-fry until golden and crisp. Serve with one of the following dip sauces to help with digestion of the oil.

Dip Sauce 1

1/2 cup water
2 to 3 tsp shoyu
1 Tbsp grated daikon

Dip Sauce 2

1/2 cup water
2 to 3 tsp shoyu
1 tsp lemon juice or natural mustard

Place the water and shoyu in a saucepan and heat. Simmer on low for 3 to 4 minutes. Turn off the flame and add either the grated daikon, lemon juice, or natural mustard. Mix and place in individual serving dishes for dipping while eating the tempura.

Noodles in Broth with Tempura

1/2 cup burdock, sliced in matchsticks
1/2 cup carrot, sliced in matchsticks
1/2 cup onion, sliced in thin half-moons
1 cup tempura batter
light sesame, sunflower, or safflower oil, for deep-frying
1 lb udon, somen, or soba, cooked, rinsed, and drained
4 to 5 cups water, including shiitake and kombu water, for broth
1 1/2 to 2 Tbsp shoyu, for broth
4 to 5 shiitake mushrooms, soaked, stems removed, and sliced, for broth
1 strip kombu, 2 inches long, soaked
1/4 cup scallion, sliced thin, for garnish

Place the water, shiitake, and kombu in a pot. Cover and bring to a boil. Reduce the flame to medium-low and simmer 5 to 7 minutes. Reduce the flame to low, remove the kombu, and set aside for future use. Add the shoyu, cover, and simmer another 3 to 5 minutes. Keep the broth warm while making the tempura.

Place the vegetables in a mixing bowl with the batter. Mix thoroughly. Heat 2 to 3 inches of oil in a heavy pot. When hot, spoon the batter and vegetables, 1 tablespoonful at a time, into the hot oil. Do not place more than 4 to 5 tablespoonfuls of the mixture in the oil at one time, as it may lower the temperature of the oil. When golden and crisp on one side, turn over and fry until golden on the other side. Remove each piece and drain on paper towels. Repeat until all tempura is made.

Place the cooked noodles in individual serving bowls and top each bowl with several pieces of tempura. Ladle the hot broth over the noodles and tempura. Garnish each with 1 tablespoon finely chopped scallion. You may also serve with one of the above dip sauces.

White Rice in Broth with Vegetable Tempura

4 to 5 mushrooms
4 to 5 slices of carrot, cut on a thin diagonal
4 to 5 pieces buttercup or butternut squash, sliced thin
4 to 5 green string beans, stems removed
4 to 5 sprigs parsley
2 cups tempura batter
light sesame, sunflower, or safflower oil, for deep-
   frying
5 cups cooked white rice
4 to 5 cups water, including shiitake and kombu soaking water, for broth
4 to 5 shiitake, soaked, stems removed, and quartered
1 strip kombu, 2 inches long, soaked
2 to 3 tsp shoyu, for broth
5 Tbsp grated daikon, for garnish
1/4 cup scallion, sliced thin, for garnish

Place the water, shiitake, and kombu in a pot. Cover and bring to a boil. Reduce the flame to medium-low and simmer 10 minutes. Remove kombu and set aside for future use. Reduce the flame to low and add the shoyu. Cover and simmer 3 to 5 minutes.

Heat 2 to 3 inches of oil in a heavy pot. Place the tempura batter in a mixing bowl. Dip the mushrooms in the batter and when the oil is hot, deep-fry until golden and crisp. Remove and drain. Next, deep-fry the carrot, then the squash, and finally the parsley. Remove and drain each vegetable when done.

Place 1 cup cooked white rice in each serving bowl. Top each bowl with 1 piece of each kind of tempura. Ladle the hot broth over the tempura and rice. Garnish each bowl with 1 tablespoon grated daikon and scallion.

Nori Maki (Rice Roll) Tempura

20 to 25 pieces nori maki
2 cups tempura batter
light sesame, sunflower, or safflower oil, for deep-
  frying
1/2 cup shoyu-ginger dip sauce

Heat 2 to 3 inches of oil in a heavy skillet. Dip 4 to 5 pieces of maki in the batter and deep-fry until golden brown and crisp. Remove and drain. Repeat until all maki has been deep-fried. Serve with dip sauce when eating.

5
Baked, Broiled, and Roasted Vegetables

In general, these cooking methods produce strong yang or contractive effects. Because vegetables cooked in these ways can be drying and tightening, we use them mostly on special occasions.

Baked Stuffed Mushroom Caps

    8 to 10 large mushrooms, stems removed
    1 cup whole wheat bread, cubed
    2 Tbsp onion, minced
    2 Tbsp celery, minced
    1/4 cup cooked seitan, minced
    1 tsp shoyu
    1/4 cup water
    1/4 tsp dried sage (optional)
    corn oil

Heat several drops of corn oil in a skillet. Sauté the onion 1 minute. Add the celery and seitan. Sauté 1 minute. Place in a mixing bowl with the bread cubes, shoyu, water, and sage. Stuff each mushroom with the mixture and place on an oiled baking tray. Bake at 350 degrees F. for 20 to 25 minutes until tender and juicy.

Baked Summer Squash Fish

**3 medium yellow summer squash, cut in half length-
wise
sesame oil
shoyu**

Cut diagonal slashes in the skin of the squash, about 1/8
to 1/4 inch apart and 1/8 inch deep. Then make diagonal
slashes in the opposite direction, thus creating XXX's on the
surface that resemble the scales on a fish. At the narrow end
of the squash, cut slits, one very close to the other, all the way
through the squash so that this end of the squash resembles
the tail of a fish. At the wide end of the squash, take a vegetable peeler and dig out a small hole for an eye and make a
small slit in front of the eye for a mouth. Lightly oil a baking
dish and place the squash on it. Lightly brush the squash skin
with oil. Bake at 375 degrees F. for about 15 minutes. Then
place several drops of shoyu on each piece and bake another
15 to 20 minutes until the squash is tender. Place on a serving
plate.

Baked Sweet Corn

**4 to 5 ears sweet corn, husks left on
2 umeboshi plums or 2 tsp umeboshi paste, for garnish**

Remove the silk and one or two layers of husk from each
ear of corn. Leave the remaining husks intact. Soak the ears of
corn in cold water for about 1/2 hour. Remove. Pre-heat the
oven to 375 degrees F. and place the corn in the oven. Bake
about 40 minutes or until tender. Remove and place on a serving platter. Each person can rub a little umeboshi or umeboshi paste on each ear as a garnish.

Baked Squash Halves

1 acorn, buttercup, butternut, delicata, or spaghetti
   squash, halved lengthwise
oil
shoyu

Oil a baking sheet lightly with oil. Oil the skin of the squash halves. Place the squash, cut side down, on the baking sheet. Pre-heat the oven to 375 to 400 degrees F. and place the squash in the oven. Bake for 35 to 45 minutes until tender. Turn the squash over and sprinkle a little shoyu over each piece. Bake another 5 to 10 minutes until soft. Remove and place on a serving platter. Slice in half or in thick wedges.

Baked Mixed Vegetables

2 carrots, cut in irregular shapes
1 burdock, cut on a diagonal
2 medium onions, quartered
1/2 small head green cabbage, cut in wedges
4 to 5 small taro potatoes, halved
1/2 to 3/4 cup water
pinch of sea salt
sesame oil (optional)

Lightly oil a casserole dish. Place the vegetables in the casserole, keeping each in a separate section. Add the water and sea salt. Cover and bake at 375 degrees F. for 40 to 45 minutes or until tender. Remove the cover and bake another 5 minutes or so. Remove and serve.

Vegetables such as daikon, turnip, rutabaga, Brussels sprouts, lotus root, squash, mushroom, corn, parsnip, and other round or root vegetables can be prepared in the same manner.

Baked Whole Vegetables

2 medium carrots
8 to 10 small boiling onions, peeled
5 medium taro potatoes, peeled
5 to 10 Brussel sprouts, hard stems removed
1/2 to 3/4 cup water
shoyu
sesame or corn oil (optional)

Lightly oil a large casserole dish. Add the vegetables, keeping them separate from each other. Add the water and sprinkle with a few drops of shoyu. Cover and bake at 375 degrees F. for 45 to 50 minutes. Remove the cover and bake another 5 to 10 minutes until soft. Remove and serve.

Baked Squash and Onions

2 cups butternut or buttercup squash, sliced thin
1 cup onion, sliced in thin half-moons
1/4 to 1/2 cup water
pinch of sea salt

Place the onion on the bottom of a casserole dish. Layer the squash on top. Add the pinch of salt and water. Cover and bake for 35 to 40 minutes until tender. Remove the cover and brown for 5 more minutes. Remove and serve.

Baked Squash Turkey

1 small blue hubbard squash, washed
1 loaf whole wheat bread, cubed
1 cup onion, diced
1 cup celery, diced
1 cup mushroom, diced
plain soymilk or water
shoyu

corn oil
dried sage (optional)

Cut a hole in the top of the squash about 4 to 5 inches across. Lift up the top and clean out the seeds. Lightly oil the skin of the squash and the top with a little corn oil. Pre-bake with the top off for 20 minutes at 375 degrees F. to dry the inside a little.

To prepare the stuffing, place a moderate amount of corn oil in a skillet and heat. Sauté the onion for 3 to 4 minutes. Add the celery and mushroom. Sauté for another 4 to 5 minutes. Season with several drops of shoyu. Remove and place in a mixing bowl. Add the bread cubes and mix. Add enough water or plain soymilk for a moist but not soggy stuffing. Add enough dried sage and shoyu to taste. Fill the hollow cavity of the squash and place the top back on. If there is extra stuffing, place it in an oiled casserole dish. Cover and bake separately for about 30 minutes before the squash is done. Bake the squash for 1 1/2 hours or until it becomes tender enough to poke a chopstick or bamboo skewer through the bottom or thick sides. Remove the top and bake another 10 minutes or so to dry slightly. The time needed for cooking will depend on the size and thickness of the squash. Adjust as needed. Remove the baking tray from the oven and let the squash cool slightly before lifting and placing on a serving platter. To serve, scoop out the stuffing and squash. This is a great dish for Thanksgiving and can be served with seitan or mushroom gravy.

Stuffing can also be made by combining cooked rice and wild rice, millet, or cous cous with the above vegetables. Corn bread and oyster stuffing is also nice. You may even add roasted seeds, nuts, or cooked chestnuts to your stuffing. Instead of baking a whole squash, you can cut buttercup or acorn squash in half lengthwise and stuff each half. The cooking time will be reduced to about 40 to 45 minutes in this case.

Baked Vegetables in Pastry

2 carrots (preferably long and not too thick) washed
   and tops removed
1 burdock, washed, top removed, and boiled whole in 1
   inch water for 5 minutes (remove, drain, and cool)
2 cups whole wheat pastry flour
1/8 tsp sea salt
1/8 to 1/4 cup corn oil
1/2 to 2/3 cup cold water

Mix the flour and salt in a bowl. Add the corn oil and mix well. Gradually add water until you have a ball of dough. Knead 1 to 2 minutes and place back in the bowl. Chill 20 minutes or so in the freezer. Roll the dough out on a lightly floured board or table as you would when making a pie crust. Cut the dough in lengthwise strips, wide enough to wrap around each carrot and the burdock. Wrap the dough around each vegetable and seal the ends and seams by squeezing gently with your hands.

Place on a lightly oiled cookie or baking sheet and bake at 350 degrees F. for about 25 to 30 minutes or until the crust is golden brown. Do not over-cook as the crust will become too hard. Remove the baking sheet from the oven and allow the vegetables to cool. Place on a cutting board. Slice each roll in half. Then slice each half in half. Then slice each quarter in half. You should now have about 12 pieces of pastry-covered vegetable rolls about 1 to 1 1/2 inches long. Place on a serving platter.

As a variation, leftover hijiki or arame sea vegetable and vegetables and vegetables can be spread on the rolled out pastry dough and rolled up in a spiral or strudel form. Seal the ends shut with a fork. Poke several holes in the roll to let steam escape. Bake on an oiled sheet as above. Slice into 1 to 2 inch rounds as above and serve.

Parsnips are also delicious when cooked in this manner. Since they are thick at the top they have to be sliced in lengthwise strips that are about the size of carrots to reduce baking time and make the roll more uniform.

Burdock Eel

This is a very strong and hardy dish. Usually, burdock is cut in thin diagonals, dipped in batter, and deep-fried like tempura. It is then baked in a covered dish. Instead of using only burdock, you may combine burdock, carrot, and onion for a sweeter, less strong dish.

10 slices burdock, sliced on a 1/4 inch thick diagonal
20 slices carrot, sliced on a 1/4 to 1/2 inch thick diagonal
10 mushrooms, sliced in half
2 medium onions, sliced in thick wedges
2 cups tempura batter
light sesame, sunflower, or safflower oil, for deep-
  frying
water
shoyu

Dip each type of vegetable separately into the batter and deep-fry until golden brown and crisp. Remove and drain. Pat each vegetable with paper towels to remove some of the oil. When all vegetables have been deep-fried, layer the vegetables in a baking or casserole dish. Add enough water to just cover the vegetables and sprinkle with several drops of shoyu. Cover and bake at 375 degrees F. until the batter separates from the vegetables and creates a thick creamy sauce. This may take 1 to 1 1/2 hours. If necessary, at the end of cooking, season with a little more shoyu and bake, uncovered, for another 10 minutes. Remove and serve in the casserole dish.

This dish is quite oily and rich but very strengthening. It is great as an occasional treat during the winter season. It is recommended to serve a a small side dish of grated daikon as a garnish to help digest the oil.

As a variation try making tempura and layering it between layers of cooked udon noodles and baking as above for a rich warming dish.

Baked Vegetable-Stuffed Sole or Flounder

4 to 5 fillets of sole or flounder, washed
3/4 cup green beans, cut French style in lengthwise thin
  strips
1/2 cup carrot, cut in very thin matchsticks
1/4 cup slivered almonds
shoyu
lemon juice
sesame oil

Lay the fillets out on a cutting board or table and place about a quarter cup of green bean strips and carrot matchsticks at the thickest end of each fillet. Sprinkle a few slivered almonds on the vegetables. Roll the fillets up and place on a lightly oiled baking dish. Sprinkle 2 to 3 drops of shoyu and several drops of lemon juice on each fillet. Bake at 375 degrees F. for several minutes until the fish is tender and the vegetables are done. Do not over-cook as this will make the fish too tough.

As a variation steam the stuffed fillets in a flat-style steamer or a skillet with very little water for several minutes until done. Cooked grain and vegetable stuffing or bread cube and vegetable stuffing can be used instead of an all-vegetable stuffing for variety.

Broiled Stuffed Mushroom Caps

8 to 10 large mushrooms, stems removed
1/4 cup cooked seitan, minced
1 Tbsp onion, minced
1 Tbsp celery, minced
1 Tbsp carrot, minced
1 tsp parsley, chives, or scallion, finely chopped

Place the seitan and vegetables in a mixing bowl and mix. Stuff each mushroom with the mixture. Place stuffed mushrooms on an oiled baking sheet. Broil for about 7 minutes until tender and juicy.

Roasted Mixed Vegetables

> 1/2 cup mushroom, quartered
> 1/2 cup onion, sliced in thin rounds
> 1/2 cup summer squash, quartered and sliced thin
> 1/4 cup green pepper, sliced thin
> 1/4 cup sweet red pepper, sliced thin
> 1/4 cup snow peas, stems removed
> light sesame oil
> shoyu
> 1/2 tsp fresh ginger juice

Lightly oil a baking sheet. Place all vegetables on the sheet and sprinkle the ginger juice and several drops of shoyu over them. Place in the broiler and cook 5 minutes. Turn and mix the vegetables and cook another 3 to 5 minutes. Remove and place in a serving dish.

Seitan and Tempeh Shish Kebabs

> 5 to 6 fresh mushrooms, halved
> 5 to 6 small broccoli florets
> 5 to 6 slices summer squash, quartered and sliced in 1/4 inch thick pieces
> 5 to 6 cubes cooked seitan, 2 inches by 2 inches
> 5 to 6 cubes boiled tempeh, 2 inches by 2 inches
> 5 to 6 thick onion wedges
> 5 to 6 thick slices red pepper

Take bamboo or metal skewers and arrange one piece of each of the above ingredients on each skewer. Prepare the following basting sauce:

> 1/4 cup shoyu

1/2 cup water
3 Tbsp brown rice syrup
1 to 2 tsp ginger juice
1 tsp sesame oil

Mix all ingredients. Baste each of the skewered vegetables with the basting sauce and place on a baking sheet. Broil for 3 to 4 minutes. Remove and baste the vegetables again. Broil another 4 to 5 minutes or baste one more time and broil until done. The vegetables should not be overcooked but still slightly crunchy. Remove and place on a serving platter.

Other thinly sliced or par-boiled vegetables can be used instead of the above. You may also use fresh or deep-fried and boiled tofu or fresh fish chunks, shrimp, or scallops instead of seitan and tempeh. Feel free to change the basting sauce, adding natural mustard, lemon or lime juice, grated onion, minced garlic, or other seasonings.

6
Pickles and Condiments

Like cooking, pickling is a form of pre-digestion. Vegetables that are pickled begin to decompose (ferment) and release energy. They are easier to digest than raw vegetables. They also aid in digestion. Because vegetables are traditionally pickled in salt or salty seasonings, such as shoyu and umeboshi (pickled plum), they are best eaten in small amounts. About a tablespoonful of pickled vegetables can be consumed daily. Also, if pickles taste too salty, feel free to rinse them under cold water before eating.

Rutabaga Onion Shoyu Pickles

> 1/2 cup rutabaga, quartered and sliced very thin
> 1/2 cup onion, sliced in half-moons
> 3/4 cup water
> 1/4 cup shoyu

Place the vegetables in a glass jar. Mix the shoyu and water in a measuring cup and pour it over the vegetables. Place a piece of cotton cheesecloth over the mouth of the jar and fasten it to the jar with a rubber band or a piece of twine. Set the jar on a counter and let it sit overnight. In the morning, remove the cheesecloth and fasten the lid of the jar on the jar. Refrigerate until you are ready to eat the pickles. Take out a small amount of pickles when you wish and rinse before eating. Your pickles will keep for 5 to 7 days in the refrigerator.

Sweet and Sour Onion and Shiitake Pickles

1 cup onion, sliced in thin half-moons
5 shiitake mushrooms, soaked, stems removed, and
  sliced thin
3/4 cup water
1/4 cup shoyu
2 to 3 Tbsp brown rice syrup
2 Tbsp brown rice vinegar

Place the water, shoyu, and rice syrup in a saucepan with the shiitake. Bring to a boil and reduce the flame to medium-low. Simmer 10 minutes. Remove from the flame and allow to cool to room temperature. Place the onion in a glass jar. Mix the vinegar with the shiitake and shoyu. Stir and pour over the onion. Place a piece of cheesecloth on the mouth of the jar and secure with a rubber band or a piece of twine. Place on a counter and let sit overnight. Remove the cheesecloth and fasten the lid on the jar. Refrigerate until ready to eat. Rinse before eating. Keep remainder refrigerated during the week until you eat them. The pickles will keep about for 5 to 7 days.

Mixed Vegetable Shoyu-Ginger Pickles

1/4 cup onion, sliced in thin half-moons
1/4 cup carrot, sliced in thin matchsticks
1/4 cup broccoli stems, tough skin removed and sliced
  in thin matchsticks
1/4 cup daikon, sliced in thin matchsticks
3/4 cup water
1/4 cup shoyu
4 to 6 thin slices of fresh ginger

Place the vegetables and ginger slices in a jar. Mix the water and shoyu and pour over the vegetables. Tie a piece of cotton cheesecloth over the mouth of the jar or fasten with a rubber band. Set aside on a counter overnight. Remove the cheesecloth and fasten the lid on the jar. Refrigerate until ready to eat. Rinse before eating. The pickles will keep about 5 to 7 days.

Mustard, Daikon, or Turnip Green Pickles

> 1 small bunch mustard, daikon, or turnip greens, sliced in 1 inch pieces
> 1/3 cup shoyu
> 2/3 cup water
> 2 Tbsp brown rice syrup
> 2 tsp tan sesame seeds, dry-roasted
> 1 Tbsp grated ginger, remove skin before grating

Pack the greens in a jar. Pour in the sesame seeds and add the ginger. Place the water, shoyu, and rice syrup in a saucepan. Bring to a boil. Reduce the flame to low and simmer 1 to 2 minutes. Remove from the flame and allow to cool to room temperature. Pour the shoyu mixture over the greens. Cover the jar with a piece of cheesecloth and set aside overnight. Remove the cheesecloth and fasten the lid on the jar. Refrigerate until ready to eat. Rinse before eating. The pickles will keep about 5 to 7 days.

Red Radish Pickles

> 1 bunch red radishes and tops (slice radishes into thin rounds and chop the greens)
> 3/4 cup water
> 1/4 cup umeboshi vinegar

Place the radishes and tops in a jar. Mix the water and umeboshi vinegar and pour over the radishes. Fasten a piece of cotton cheesecloth on top of the jar and set aside overnight. Remove the cheesecloth and place the lid on the jar. Refrigerate until ready to eat. Rinse before eating. The pickles will keep about 5 to 7 days.

Mixed Vegetable-Ume Pickles

1/4 cup onion, sliced in thin half-moons
1/4 cup carrot, sliced in thin matchsticks
1/4 cup cauliflower, sliced in small florets and each floret sliced in half
1/4 cup broccoli stems, skin removed and sliced in thin matchsticks
3/4 cup water
1/4 cup umeboshi vinegar

Place the vegetables in a jar. Mix the water and umeboshi vinegar and pour over the vegetables. Fasten a piece of cotton cheesecloth on the top of the jar and set aside overnight. Remove the cheesecloth and place the lid on the jar. Refrigerate until ready to eat. Rinse before eating. The pickles will keep about 5 to 7 days.

Ginger Pickles

1/2 cup ginger slices, skin removed, sliced very thin, and blanched 1/2 minute
1/4 cup umeboshi vinegar
3/4 cup water
2 to 3 shiso leaves
2 to 3 Tbsp brown rice syrup
1 Tbsp brown rice vinegar

Place the ginger and shiso leaves in a jar. Place the water, umeboshi vinegar, and rice syrup in a saucepan and bring to a boil. Reduce the flame to low and simmer 1 to 2 minutes. Remove from the flame and cool to room temperature. Mix the brown rice vinegar with the ume vinegar solution and pour over the ginger. Cover the top of the jar with cotton cheesecloth and set aside overnight. Remove the cheesecloth and fasten the lid on the jar. Refrigerate until ready to eat. Rinse before eating. Keep remaining pickles refrigerated until ready to eat. The pickles will last about 5 to 7 days

Daikon-Sauerkraut Pickles

1/2 cup daikon, sliced in thin half-moons
1/2 cup prepared, organic sauerkraut
1/2 to 3/4 cup sauerkraut juice

Place the daikon and sauerkraut in a jar, packing it down firmly with your fingers or a wooden pestle. Pour the sauerkraut juice over the daikon and sauerkraut. Fasten a piece of cotton cheesecloth on the top of the jar. Set aside overnight. Remove cheesecloth and fasten the lid on the jar. Refrigerate until ready to eat. These pickles are very mild and do not usually need to be rinsed unless you are on a low salt diet. Keep remaining pickles refrigerated until ready to eat. These pickles will keep about 5 to 7 days.

Daikon-Lemon Pickles

1 daikon, 10 to 12 inches long, sliced in thin matchsticks
3 to 4 pieces lemon rind, about 2 inches long by 1/4 inch thick
1 1/2 tsp sea salt

Place the daikon in a small ceramic pickle crock and evenly mix in the salt. Place the lemon rind in with the daikon. Place a small saucer or wooden dish down inside the crock, resting on the daikon. Fill a jar with water and set it down inside the crock on top of the saucer. Remove the lemon rind after 4 hours or the lemon flavor will overpower the daikon. Place the saucer and jar back in the crock on top of the daikon. Set in a cool place for 1 to 2 days. They are now ready to eat. Refrigerate to store. Remove as needed and rinse before eating. These pickles will keep about one week.

Turnip-Kombu Pickles

3 medium-sized turnips, sliced in thin rounds or half-moons
2 to 3 strips kombu, 6 to 8 inches long, soaked
2 to 3 Tbsp sea salt

Roll up each piece of kombu into a round cylinder and slice in very thin strips or matchsticks. Sprinkle a small amount of sea salt on the bottom of a ceramic pickle crock. Layer the turnip, kombu, and sea salt in alternating layers in the crock, making sure that the last layer on top is sea salt. Place a saucer down inside the crock. Fill a jar with water and place the top on it. Place the jar down inside the crock on top of the saucer for weight. Let sit for 8 to 10 hours. Water should rise up to the disk. Pour off and place the saucer and water jar back in the crock. Let sit in a cool place for 1 to 2 days. The kombu makes these pickles slippery. This is normal. Refrigerate to store. Rinse before eating. These pickles will keep about 1 week.

Salt Brine Pickles

3 cups water
2 to 3 tsp sea salt
2 pickling cucumbers, quartered
1/2 red onion, sliced in half-moons
1/2 cup cauliflower florets, sliced in half
1/2 cup carrot, cut in matchsticks

Place the water and sea salt in a saucepan and bring to a boil. Reduce the flame to low and simmer 1 minute. Remove from the flame and allow to cool to room temperature. Place the vegetables in a glass jar and pour the brine solution over them. Cover the top with cheesecloth and keep in a cool place for 2 to 3 days. Remove cheesecloth and place the lid on top of the jar. Refrigerate to store. Rinse before eating. These pickles will keep about 2 weeks.

Cucumber-Miso Pickles

1 cup barley miso
1/4 cup cucumber, sliced in rounds

Tie the sliced cucumber up in a thin layer of cheesecloth. Insert into a jar of miso, completely covering the sack. Let sit for 1 day. Remove the sack. Remove the cucumber slices from the sack and rinse. They are now ready to eat. Any very thinly sliced vegetables or even apples may be pickled in miso.

Quick Pickled Chinese Cabbage

3 cup Chinese cabbage, sliced
1 to 1 1/2 tsp sea salt

Mix the salt in with the Chinese cabbage and place in a ceramic pickle crock. Place a saucer down inside the crock resting on the cabbage. Fill a jar with water and place it on top of the saucer for weight. Let sit in a cool place for 2 to 3 days. Refrigerate to store. Rinse before eating. These will keep about 5 to 7 days.

Miso-Scallion Condiment

1 cup scallion or chives, sliced thin
scallion roots, minced
1 Tbsp barley miso, puréed
2 to 3 Tbsp water
1 tsp light or dark sesame oil

Heat the oil in a skillet and sauté the scallion roots several seconds. Place the scallion tops in the skillet. Add the miso and water and mix. Cover the skillet, reduce the flame to low, and simmer for about 5 minutes or so. Place in a condiment dish.

Onion and Green Pepper-Miso Condiment

    1 cup onion, sliced in thin half-moons
    1 cup green pepper, seeds removed and sliced thin
    1 to 1 1/2 Tbsp barley miso, puréed
    1/4 cup water
    1 tsp dark sesame oil

Heat the oil in a skillet and sauté the onion for 2 to 3 minutes. Add the pepper and sauté another 3 to 4 minutes. Add the miso and water and mix. Cover the skillet and cook over a low flame for 7 to 10 minutes, checking occasionally to make sure there is enough liquid. Remove and place in a serving dish.

Grated Daikon Condiment

    1/4 cup grated daikon
    1 Tbsp scallion, chopped fine
    several drops shoyu

Spoon 1 tablespoonful of grated daikon onto your plate. Sprinkle chopped scallion on top. Pour 1 to 3 drops shoyu on top of each serving. This condiment is wonderful when eating fish, mochi, or oily food. As a variation try grated daikon and carrot with scallion, nori strips, and shoyu.

Sweet Vegetable-Miso Condiment

    1/4 cup onion, diced
    1/4 cup carrot, diced
    1/4 cup winter squash, diced
    1/4 cup cabbage, diced
    1 Tbsp barley miso, puréed
    1/4 cup water
    1 tsp light or dark sesame oil

Heat the oil in a skillet and sauté the onion for 1 to 2 minutes. Add the other vegetables and sauté 2 to 3 minutes. Add the water and miso. Mix and cover the skillet. Cook over a low flame for about 7 to 10 minutes. Place in a serving dish.

Resources

One Peaceful World is an international information network and friendship society devoted to the realization of one healthy, peaceful world. Activities include educational and spiritual tours, assemblies and forums, international food aid and development, and publishing. Membership is $30/year for individuals and $50 for families and includes a subscription to the One Peaceful World Newsletter and a free book from One Peaceful World Press. For further information, contact:

One Peaceful World
Box 10, Becket, MA 01223
(413) 623–2322
Fax (413) 623–8827

The Kushi Institute offers ongoing classes and seminars including cooking classes and workshops presented by Wendy Esko. For information, contact:

Kushi Institute
Box 7, Becket MA 01223
(413) 623–5741
Fax (413) 623–8827

Recommended Reading

Books by Wendy Esko

1. *Aveline Kushi's Wonderful World of Salads* (Japan Publications, 1989).
2. *The Changing Seasons Cookbook* (with Aveline Kushi, Avery Publishing Group, 1985).
3. *Diet for Natural Beauty* (with Aveline Kushi, Japan Publications, 1991).
4. *The Good Morning Macrobiotic Breakfast Book* (with Aveline Kushi, Avery Publishing Group, 1991).
5. *Introducing Macrobiotic Cooking* (Japan Publications, 1978).
6. *The Macrobiotic Cancer Prevention Cookbook* (with Aveline Kushi, Avery Publishing Group, 1988).
7. *Macrobiotic Cooking for Everyone* (with Edward Esko, Japan Publications, 1980).
8. *Macrobiotic Family Favorites* (with Aveline Kushi, Japan Publications, 1987).
9. *Macrobiotic Pregnancy and Care of the Newborn* (with Michio and Aveline Kushi and Edward Esko, Japan Publications, 1984).
10. *The New Pasta Cuisine* (with Aveline Kushi, Japan Publications, 1992).
11. *The Quick and Natural Macrobiotic Cookbook* (with Aveline Kushi, Contemporary Books, 1989).
12. *Raising Healthy Kids* (with Michio and Aveline Kushi and Edward Esko, Avery Publishing Group, 1994).
13. *Rice Is Nice* (One Peaceful World Press, 1995).
14. *Soup du Jour* (One Peaceful World Press, 1996).
15. *Whole Grain Cookbook* (with Aveline Kushi, Japan Publications, 1996.

About the Author

Wendy Esko teaches macrobiotic ocoking at the Kushi Institute and around the world. She is the author of *Introducing Macrobiotic Cooking*, co-author with Aveline Kushi of *The Changing Seasons Macrobiotic Cookbook*, and author of *Rice Is Nice, Soup du Jour*, and many other books. She lives with her husband, Edward, a macrobiotic author and teacher, and eight children in Becket, Massachusetts.

Recipe Index

Corn Meal-Fried Summer Squash or Zucchini, 49
Corn on the Cob, 30
Creamed Corn and Fresh Lima Beans, 30
Crushed Burdock with Sesame Vinaigrette, 23
Cucumber-Miso Pickles, 86

Daikon-Lemon Pickles, 84
Daikon-Sauerkraut Pickles, 84
Deep-Fried Corn Fritters, 59
Deep-Fried Fish and Vegetable Balls, 59
Deep-Fried Lotus Root Dumplings, 63
Deep-Fried Squash and Chestnut Balls, 58
Deep-Fried Squash Balls, 57
Deep-Fried Vegetable Chips, 56
Dried Daikon and Vegetables, 29

Ginger Pickles, 83
Glazed Carrots, 31
Grated Daikon Condiment, 87
Green Beans Almondine, 48
Green Beans with Sesame-Miso Dressing, 24

Kinpira, 45

Marinated Lotus Root Salad, 40
Marinated Daikon and Carrot Salad, 41
Miso-Apple Dressing, 43
Miso-Scallion Condiment, 86
Mixed Vegetable Shoyu-Ginger Pickles, 81
Mixed Vegetable-Ume Pickles, 83
Mustard, Daikon, or Turnip Green Pickles, 82

New England Boiled Dinner, 31
Noodles in Broth with Tempura, 67
Nori Maki Tempura, 69

Onion and Green Pepper-Miso Condiment, 87

Pan-Fried Parsnip, 47

Pressed Red Radish, 39
Pressed Salad with Sea Salt and Brown Rice Vinegar, 38
Pressed Salad with Sea Salt, 37
Pressed Salad with Umeboshi Vinegar, 38
Puréed Squash Aspic, 42

Quick Pickled Chinese Cabbage, 86
Quick Sautéed Greens, 44

Red and Green Coleslaw, 39
Red Radish Pickles, 82
Red Radishes with Umeboshi-Kuzu Sauce, 27
Roasted Mixed Vegetables, 78
Rutabaga-Onion Shoyu Pickles, 80

Salt Brine Pickles, 85
Sautéed Brussel Sprouts and Walnuts, 54
Sautéed Glazed Baby Carrots, 49
Sautéed Lotus Root, 55
Sautéed Mushrooms and Garlic, 47
Sautéed Onion and Seitan in Mustard Sauce, 51
Sautéed Pepper with Miso, 50
Sautéed Squash and Onions, 47
Scrambled Tofu and Vegetables, 53
Seafood Oden, 33
Seitan and Tempeh Shish Kebabs, 78
Seitan and Vegetable Balls, 60
Steamed Greens, 15
Steamed Stuffed Squash, 16
Steamed Summer Squash, 15
Steamed Whole Onions with Shiitake-Kuzu Gravy, 16
Steamed Winter Squash, 15
Stir-Fried Chinese Vegetables in Kuzu Sauce, 52
Stir-Fried Portabello Mushroom and Broccoli Rabe, 50
Stir-Fried Savoy Cabbage with Black Sesame Seeds, 53
Sukiyaki, 34
Summer Nabe, 32
Summer Nishime, 25
Sweet and Sour Onion and Shiitake Pickles, 81

Macrobiotic Cooking Series
By Wendy Esko

*108 Quick and Easy
Brown Rice Recipes*

Wendy Esko
Foreword by Gale Jack

*Healthy Homemade Soups
for All Seasons*

Wendy Esko
Foreword by Gale Jack

Vol. 1
Rice Is Nice

Vol. 2
Soup du Jour

Vol. 3
Eat Your Veggies

Each Volume $8.95
Special Set of 3 Books: $21.95 Save 20%
Enclose $3.00 for shipping and handling per order

Send check, money order, or Visa/MC # and expiration date to:
One Peaceful World Press, Box 10, Becket, MA 01223
(413) 623-2322 • Fax (413) 623-8827